Sis,
   without the
cyber sis I could have never
come this far.
   I thank you for listening to my
broken heart so many times.
   I Love You Sis!
      Lola Cross

Kathy Kellum, my Cwazy & Wonderful Sis

SHE BLEW HIM STRAIGHT TO HEAVEN

The True Story of Troy Patton

By
Lola Cross

Text © Lola Cross 2007.

Paper back:
ISBN-10: 0-9795276-0-0
EAN13: 978-0-9795276-0-9

Hard back:
ISBN-10: 0-9795276-1-9
EAN13: 978-0-9795276-1-6

Interior formatting/cover design by
Rend Graphics 2007
www.rendgraphics.com

Published by:

rendpub

Rend Publishing 2007
www.rendpublishing.com

To order additional copies, please visit:
www.rendpublishing.com
or
www.Amazon.com

DEDICATION

This book is dedicated first and foremost to the person who's life and death inspired me (along with his sister Lori pushing me) into writing it. Troy Evan Patton, our beautiful son, brother, daddy, uncle, nephew, grandson and friend to so many.

It's also dedicated to his beautiful daughters Britany and Jessica as it is through them, he will live on.

And to the future generations that will not have the pleasure of knowing their Grandpa Troy, their Great Uncle, their friend who could have been. There are so many people that have yet to be born that are going to be missing so much by not knowing Troy. I hope this book helps them to get an idea of what a special man he was.

I also dedicate this book to Troy's dad Bill, his sister Lori and his brother Todd. Without all of you loving Troy as I did, he would not have been molded into the kind soul that he was.

Last but not least, my husband Larry and Bill's wife Bernie. You have both stood by us through this unspeakable tragedy and our over powering anguish. There had to be times you had to be at a loss as to what to do or say, as you watched our hearts shatter with sorrow in front of your very eyes. I know at times Larry felt that his wife died the same day Troy left us. But, in spite of the grief that only a parent who has lost a child can understand, you stood by us and still are standing by us. Bill and I thank you for being there for us.

ACKNOWLEDGEMENTS

This is the first and most likely the last book I will ever write. I wrote it because I felt Troy deserved to have his story told.

I acknowledge that I write this book with the blessings of my family, which includes my children, husband, ex-husband and his wife and my grandchildren. In some instances they shared their own feelings and also helped me to recall the time frame and dates of different occasions or incidents.

Thank you all for having faith in me.

This book is not written by an author. The words written in this book come straight from the heart of a grieving mom to these pages. If you look closely, you may see my tear stains. I know you will feel them.

INTRODUCTION

Garth Brooks released his signature song 'The Dance' on April 12th, 1989. The words to that song go as follows.

Looking back
On the memory of
The dance we shared
Beneath the stars above

For a moment
all the world was right
How could I have known
that you'd ever say goodbye

and now
I'm glad I didn't know
the way it all would end
the way it all would go

Our lives
are better left to chance

I coulda missed the pain
but, I'da had to miss the dance

Troy, you were an awesome addition to our family and to all the lives you touched in your almost thirty-five years. Even though our hearts are shattered that you were taken from us in such a horrific way and our pain runs deeper than imaginable, none of us that loved you so very much would have wanted to miss the dance.

CHAPTER

1

The First Day Of The Rest Of His Life

"Your lives as you knew them have just changed on this day... forever." Those were Dr. Goode's words to us.

If I had known in 1970 or even 1965 what I know now, would I have changed anything? Maybe. I might have changed some things... but, I wouldn't have changed having my babies.

Lori and Todd came very close together. Bill and I were married on May 29th, 1965. Lori was born on February 9th, 1966 and Todd came along on January 30th, 1967 missing my birthday by one day and beating Lori's first birthday by ten days. I hadn't planned on having them less than a year apart and it broke my heart to go to the hospital in labor with Todd which meant leaving my daughter with my sister for three or four days. The fact that Lori began walking during that short time I was in the hospital didn't make me feel any better. She seemed like she had aged by three years when my sister put her down and she came toddling across the floor to me with her tiny hands raised in the air holding onto those invisible sky hooks that all little one's use in the beginning to keep their balance. Wow! I couldn't stop the tears. My baby girl was walking and I missed it happening.

On the bright side of things, labor with Todd was much easier than when I had Lori... but, why not? Nothing had time to get back in place before I was pregnant that second time. It was pretty shocking to me back then, but I always said later that if I had it to do over, I'd have them that close in age again. And I would. It was kind of like raising twins. Many people asked me if they were twins, because they looked so much alike by the time Todd was reaching his one year mark. The blonde hair, blue eyes, the Patton hands and feet. If I hadn't known better I would have wondered if I had anything to do with their births. I loved my babies, both of them, but since I wasn't keen on the idea of having three in less than three years, I went on birth control. And I did this with the blessing of their dad, who after Lori was born had an aversion to me going on the pill. Less than three months later I was pregnant again with Todd. So, even though Bill loved our babies, after January 30th, 1967 his objections to birth control had softened... totally.

I loved being a mom. I loved the pitter-patter of little feet in the house. Most days, I even found humor and something to smile about in the squabbles that would occasionally break out between big sister and little brother. It was all a part of being mom and a part of sibling rivalry. I remember when Lori used to trade Todd a toy for his bottle after she had already been taken off the bottle. Of course, Todd who was then and still is a very gentle soul didn't cry over his lost bottle, because he had some wonderful toy to distract him from the bottle that Lori was sucking down so quickly before mom came in and saw her.

They really were such good babies and every place we took them people complimented us on how well behaved our children were. And it wasn't because we threatened them with bodily harm or anything. They just seemed to naturally be of good nature. I guess while they had the Patton blonde hair, blue eyes, feet and hands they had the Taylor (my maiden name) dispositions. *smile* They were just good children... no doubt about it.

And they were smart. Lori watched Sesame Street

every day and I was shocked and amazed at the way she learned from watching that show. I remember one time she said she could tie her shoe. I said, "Okay, show me how you tie your shoe." not really believing she could. And she did it! I hadn't taught her that and neither had her dad. Another day she sat down at the table (before she was even in Kindergarten) and proceeded to write her A B C's. I was bursting with pride. What a smart girl she was! It seems she learned this all from Sesame Street and it wasn't long until she had also taught Todd to do the same things. They were quite the team, the two of them. I was so proud of my beautiful babies.

Bill and I did a lot of moving when we were first married. We started out living in Delavan, the town where I grew up but soon moved to Pekin. Things were always strained with my mom and I so I thought I wanted to move away. We lived in an apartment for a while in Pekin and I wanted to move back to Delavan. My sister, my brother, my grandma and my parents were all there. And I got homesick for my hometown. It seemed we moved back and forth from Pekin to Delavan a few different times. Then one day, after spending every weekend in Havana while Bill fished with a man he met through his job, we decided to move to there. That was the summer of 1969. It seemed that Havana was the place we were meant to be. We both liked it here and we had already met many people before moving here. I told Bill that we had to make up our mind if this is where we wanted to raise our children, because once Lori started school there would be no moving from town to town. So, Havana became our new 'permanent' home and our children's 'hometown' where they would grow up, go to school, make lifelong friendships and bond with the people of the Community.

In 1970 it began to sink in that soon both Lori and Todd would be going to school and I would be home alone without the laughter and the giggles of little ones running through the house. I was still on the birth control I started at twenty years old after Todd was born and I would soon be twenty-four. I thought about it a lot and then talked with Bill. I wanted to have a third child. I didn't care if it was a girl or boy, I just wanted to have another baby. Bill agreed with me, I think without any argument at all. I went off the pill in June of 1970 thinking that it would take me probably six months to even get pregnant. That's what the Doctor's would tell you back then. WRONG!. I never had another period. I was pregnant just thinking about it, I think. I always said, if not for birth control I would have had a child for every month of the year and maybe double for some months, since twins did run in the family. I was happy... I was gonna have a little one again. I did go through some morning sickness (which usually lasted all day) which was annoying. I played it down mainly because I didn't want Lori and Todd to hate this baby before it was even born because they would think it caused mom to be sick all the time. Fortunately that part of it passed quickly and I felt good through out the rest of my pregnancy.

I can remember talking with Lori and Todd about the fact that there was going to be three of them and asked them what they thought would make good names for a boy or a girl... whichever it might be. Their choices... Pebbles for a girl and BamBam for a boy. Can we say the Flintstones were popular back then?? Actually, in hindsight... BamBam might have been a pretty suitable name for the little bundle of joy that was about to make it's identity known to the world.

Silly me. I thought, "Todd was my second child and the labor was a breeze. I played Double Solitaire with Bill clear up until they wheeled me into delivery. This was my 3rd child and would certainly be even easier labor because everyone said your third one was the easiest." WRONG AGAIN!

My mom and dad came down on March 4th, 1971 to see me because they knew I'd be having the baby any day. That's the day I told my dad that if the baby was a boy he would be named Troy Evan. My dad cried, because Evan was his middle name and at that time he did not have a child or grandchild with his name. My mom even hugged me when they left that day. It was the first time I ever remembered her hugging me. That's a whole other story that I don't care to get into now. Regardless of the hugs and the tears, I went into labor later that day. By ten o'clock that Thursday night, I knew it was time to take my two oldest (but still my babies) to my girlfriend's house so I could get to the hospital.

Labor went on and on and on. I was starting to think they were going to let me and this unborn baby die before they ever did anything. I was in labor all night Thursday, all day Friday, all night Friday and by Saturday morning March 6th I was totally exhausted and scared. I really was scared for the well being of my unborn baby. Whoever said the third child is the easiest to have is so full of it. Don't believe any of those old wives tales. They are lies! Gosh, I was frustrated. No, I wasn't frustrated.

I was downright angry! I wanted this baby to be born and I wanted it to be born NOW! I couldn't handle any more never mind that poor child waiting to meet this big ol' world out here.

I was getting very scared, very exhausted and very, very angry and sick of being in pain. I guess they didn't have epidurals back then, because I sure didn't get one. I would have traded my husband off for an epidural at that point, if I had ever heard of one. Seems women in long labor, get a bit testy.

It had started snowing early that morning. I mean really, really snowing. It was piling up fast. Bill, trying to keep my mind off the excruciating labor which I was convinced was going to kill both me and my baby said, "Boy, look at that snow out there." You don't EVEN want to know what I said back to him. Poor guy.

They have not a clue what labor feels like, because if they did... our species would very likely be extinct or close enough that we'd be on the endangered species list. The whales might be marching in protests to save *us*.

I really don't know why he hung around for as long as he did, except that he probably feared I'd rip his arm from the socket if he tried to leave. Finally around 11:45 a.m. or maybe a bit later... he decided that he would go get a bite to eat in the cafeteria. "Sure, go ahead and get something to eat while I'm lying here dying. You'll need your strength to bury me." Sounded like he had lots of time to eat since the Nurse had just checked and said I was still not dilating. Oh my gosh... would this labor never end? I knew in my heart that none of this was Bill's fault and in spite of my bad mood (putting it mildly), I knew he needed to eat something and I also knew that he needed a break from this horror flick he had been thrown into. So, I gave him permission to leave me on my death bed and go get something to eat downstairs. He had no sooner left and I could tell that something was changing and changing quickly. The nurse came in, looked and yelled out... "she's having the baby" and they whisked me off to the delivery room. Wow... all those hours and suddenly when I dilated, it just happened so quickly. I should have sent Bill to lunch on Thursday night about midnight. He was gone just a short time and when he came back the Doctor had the Nurse open the door to the Delivery Room and he said to Bill, "Meet your son Mr. Patton." Bill almost fainted from the sight of a newborn baby and all that goes along with it. He would have never made a good doctor or even midwife. What am I saying? He couldn't have even been on the cleaning crew that cleans the delivery rooms. Anything bright red that came from a person's body makes him very pale and very, very faint. He almost passed out when they took my blood for the blood tests when we got married.

After all the pain, the frustration and the anger my little guy made it into this big ol' world at 12:20 p.m. on a snowy Saturday, March 6th, 1971 and he stole my heart the minute I saw him. Actually, he had stolen my heart before I even knew he was a 'he.' There he was... all six pounds four ounces of him and he was nineteen and a half inches long. How could someone so tiny and so sweet cause so much pain? But, one of the old wives tales I found to be true is the one where they say, "as soon as you hold that baby in your arms, you realize it was worth all the pain."

I held him close to me and I thought to myself,

"World, I'd like you to meet our son, Troy Evan Patton. My sweet baby." Staring at his tiny face and hands I said, "I will love you and take care of you and protect you from the things in this world that can hurt you. I promise you that my sweet boy."

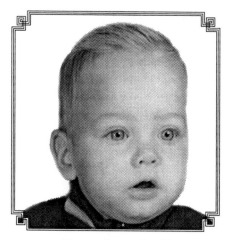

Troy at six months old

CHAPTER

The Joy Of Troy

2

WOW! That's the first word that comes to mind when I think of my sweet baby boy. He was an awesome baby. So very good and such a happy baby from the start. He was so cute and so tiny and so much of a blessing that I wanted to just sit and watch him sleep (which I found myself doing all the time) and as he made little faces, twisting his mouth first one way then the other and stretching and wriggling. He looked just like one of those life-like dolls. He was beautiful. He wasn't red and wrinkled. His skin was smooth with a beautiful complexion and brassy red-orange hair. He was absolutely perfect. I was good at having perfect babies, because Lori and Todd were perfect too. Well they were! Of course, it wasn't long until he had blonde hair (although his hair was never quite as thick as Lori and Todd's) and the most gorgeous blue eyes you ever saw. All of my children have blue eyes, but Troy's was just a tad bit different. I'm not sure what it was. It was like they had a light that shown from within... a fluorescent blue light that absolutely melted my heart when combined with that smile of his. And of course, along with the blue eyes and blonde hair, he also had the Patton feet and hands. But, much to my pleasure, he also had that 'Taylor Disposition' that made all three of my children so special. Oh what a precious child he was and he was OURS. Ours to love and to take care of and to protect for as long as we lived. His dad and I.

And Lori and Todd? Oh how they loved their little brother! They found him to be very funny and loved to watch him make faces and wriggle around as much as I did, I think. Lori—she was the 'mother hen' way back then and she would hold him on her lap with a pillow while watching cartoons and let him suck HER finger. It kept him content, made her feel good, and gave me the chance to get supper on the table each late afternoon. How lucky can one woman be? I had three beautiful blue eyed, blonde haired babies... with my intellect and disposition. *smile*

By the time Troy was able to sit up and began crawling, he had become Lori and Todd's personal living doll to play house with. He got pushed in the stroller and sat in the playpen and lugged around while they pretended to be mom and dad and he was their baby. It was so much fun to watch them and he was so happy to oblige them in being their own personal toy. There was no doubt about it, Troy was loved by the whole family and he was a true blessing to us all.

Then there were our friends. The ones we had met even before moving here, the one's we met after moving here and the one's we had yet to meet. Eventually, they would all love Troy as he became a part of their lives. There just wasn't any way that you could keep from loving that boy. It was just the way he was. He was cute. He was funny. He was ornery... that was obvious. But with a twinkle in his eye and a wonderful smile—he was good and he was sweet. He was as sweet as they come and everyone could see that. They all loved him for all the funny things he did, even as a small toddler. They loved him because of his sweet disposition. He became special not to just his family, but to our friends. I don't think any of us realized just how much he was loved by everyone, and I'm certain that Troy did not know.

When he was a toddler, he had some eccentricities that you might not expect a three or four year old to have. For one thing, he hated new clothes and new shoes! It was like pulling teeth to get him to wear anything new! He would take his new shoes and hide them so he wouldn't have to wear them. One time in the store a very dear friend and a true buddy to Troy wanted to buy him a little red baseball jacket. This perfect little boy of mine threw the biggest fit in that store that you would ever see. I was so embarrassed. He did not want that new coat tried on him and he fought it until he was just too tired to fight it anymore I guess. Finally, Tex got it on him and it fit, so he bought it for him. In the beginning, Troy wouldn't wear it. Then once he finally did wear it, he didn't want to take it off. EVER! He hung onto that coat for about three years at least I think. Actually, much to my surprise, when he was in first grade he came home from school with his school pictures and , oh my gosh... he had taken that coat (which was by then, three sizes too small) to school and had his picture taken in it. I was mortified but at the same time couldn't stop laughing. To this very day that is one of our very favorite pictures of him—Troy in the little red coat with the sleeves only reaching half way down his arms. His little hands were folded in front of him, an angelic grin on his face and with that twinkle in his eye, that appeared to be saying, "Boy, this picture will be great, cause I love this coat!" Today, if you offered me a million dollars for that picture, I wouldn't take it and neither would his dad.

There was another thing he used to do, and I still think of it all the time. If he ever fell and bumped his head or banged his knee or whatever, he would always say something like, "Why did you put that there, Mom?"

"Well Troy, sorry but the house came built with that window sill."

21

And if he went to eat a meal and it had just come off the stove, he would let me know that I cooked it too hot. He did NOT like baths when he was a toddler. Many times the first words out of his mouth of a morning were , "Do I have to take a bath tonight?" Only, he never sounded grouchy or even like a spoiled brat. It was just Troy asking or saying whatever he was thinking in a quiet, matter-of-fact manner.

He talked and walked in his sleep. Sometimes he would scare me if I would be up late and suddenly there was Troy with his eyes open, walking into the room saying something that made no sense, because he actually was sound asleep. One of my fears was that he would walk in his sleep and get out the door while I was sleeping and I wouldn't hear him. But, that never happened and he did grow out of the sleep walking phase.

He was cuddly in those first years of his life. I can still see him climbing out of bed, coming to the kitchen and I'd lift him into my lap. He'd pull his little legs up and just sit there cuddling with me while Lori and Todd ate their breakfast and got off to school. His little head lying against my chest and my arms wrapped around him. Most days he would remain sitting there on my lap long after they had left for school. I relished every moment I had like that with him. When I close my eyes now and think of it, I can almost feel him in my lap just like those times from many years ago.

Everyone, and I do mean everyone, spoiled and teased our Troy. He was just so much fun to wrestle, joke, and horse around with. Everyone loved him and they would do everything they could to get him to do something or say something funny and cute—which I have to say, didn't take much. It sometimes seemed that everything he did or said was funny and cute. He seemed to become the nucleus of our family, the hub of our circle of friends. Even Lori and Todd made him the focus of their attention most days. They found him to be very amusing on the days he wasn't being a pain in the tush. He thought he should be able to do everything they could do.

Troy had many grown up buddies, but his very favorite was Tex. And Tex is still to this day one of the orneriest, fun loving people I know. He used to get Troy into so much mischief, and he loved every minute of it. He would just throw his head back and laugh when he had just gotten Troy to drop his drawers and pee out in the back yard, or worse yet... down over the embankment at the baseball field. Good grief, what he didn't think of to tell Troy to do wasn't worth thinking of. I remember one time we were all in our back yard getting ready to cook out. Troy was small and was into the potty training stage. He said he had to pee.

Tex said, "Hey buddy, just pee right out here in the yard. Nobody is looking."

Troy always listened to Tex and nobody was looking *except* for the ten to twelve people who were out there for the cook out. Down went the pants and there went the stream of pee straight up into the air and right back down onto Troy's head. He got this confused look on his face like, "Hey, where's that coming from?" while still peeing and looking straight up into the mysterious water that was hitting him in the face and head. Tex was just howling and the rest of us were too. It lead to Troy getting one of those dreaded baths. He was so young that I don't think at that time he ever figured out where that water was coming from and why we were all laughing so hard. Years later he would grin and his face would turn red when that story would get told over and over.

The kids and I used to have cleaning parties on a Friday night. We'd turn the music up loud and we'd dust and mop and vacuum and just have a good ol' time making the chores more enjoyable. I always taught my children how to clean house and believe me, my daughter in laws appreciated it a lot in later years. Troy wasn't much help way back then, but boy he liked singing to those songs we had blaring while dancing around the house with a dust rag in our hand. He especially liked Delta Dawn, and that little guy... when he was not peeing in the yard would sit on the potty and sing that song at the top of his lungs. Todd, Lori and I and anyone else within ear shot would bust a gut laughing when he was singing his song while having his daily constitutional—without our little serenader knowing, of course. I can hear him singing that song like it happened yesterday. I wonder when he grew up if he ever caught himself humming that song while in the bathroom? That makes me smile to think about it.

Troy used to laugh at me for crying over movies, books or songs. All my kids did really, even though many times watching *Little House On The Prairie*, they all teared up too.

When the kids were young we always watched *Laura Ingalls, The Waltons, Eight Is Enough*—all those family shows. *Happy Days*! They might see me crying watching any of them... not might... they would. Heck, as soon as the music started turning sentimental and the crying part would start, Troy would turn around and watch me, because he knew the tears would start. The little stinker.

One time we were watching *Eight Is Enough*. I have it on VHS, actually. It was their Christmas special and Tommy was having a really hard time dealing with the death of his mother. Each year she had always found something really special for one of the kids during the year and then wrapped it and put it away somewhere until Christmas. This particular show they found a gift for Tommy from his mother, that she had bought before she died. Oh my God! When they gave him that book and the dad read what she wrote to Tommy, I just began to cry so hard. I was sobbing! I couldn't stop the tears and my kids were cracking up at me and I had to go to the bathroom and regain my composure. It was the most moving and emotional thing I had ever witnessed on that show. Every year at Christmas, including this Christmas I would be asked if I wanted to watch the *Eight Is Enough* Christmas special. Troy was so ornery. He'd tease me about crying over commercials—usually just Folger's or Hallmark commercials.

Gosh... those were good times sitting there eating popcorn with my kids and watching all those family shows. We ate popcorn every night of the week, I think. My ex used to tell us he didn't see how we could stand popcorn every night.

When Todd was in the service and stationed away from home in Sicily, Nicki asked him to make popcorn one night and he couldn't do it, because it made him too homesick. Troy used to make popcorn for his girls, because they had all grew up on the popcorn you pop in a pan on the stove and cover with butter. There wasn't any microwave popcorn in our house then. Heck, maybe microwaves hadn't been invented, yet.

Troy used to ask me how much eggs were when I was a kid, because he thought I grew up in Walnut Grove with Laura Ingall's.

Troy's dad was an avid fisherman even before we moved to Havana. And actually we all became lovers of fishing. Troy was going on camping trips before he could even walk. He grew up with fishing in his blood and he never gave up his love of the sport.

The fishing trips with my children were so much fun and I loved it! If Lori would get a fish on her hook, she would be squealing and jumping around yelling, "Oh Lordy, Lordy! I got a fish. I got a fish!" She would get so excited that I don't know how she managed to pull them in, but she did. She was hilarious to watch and I used to pray for her to get a fish on her hook so I could watch her go nuts over it. It used to crack me up when Todd and Troy would go wandering the banks. I used to tell them they were like fishing with Gilligan. Todd wasn't one to just sit in one spot fishing, usually. He would always be walking around trying to find the spot where that big one was just waiting for the worm on his hook. Of course, Troy would follow his brother around, since he didn't really like sitting still either. Now me, I was content to sit in one spot and hope that I didn't get too many bites to interrupt the peaceful feeling that fishing gave me. Besides, I didn't want to miss anything funny my children might do. And Bill... poor Bill. When the kids were really young he spent many times untangling lines or tying hooks and sinkers back on the lines because the kids could find any rock and tree branch under water, just as if they had radar zoned in on it. If it was there... one of them would get their line tangled in it. Guaranteed!

Fishing is a good sport for a family. It's a way to spend some quality time with each other and a good time to just talk and relax and discuss anything you want. That is if you don't have your line wrapped around a tree in the water. I loved, loved, loved our fishing outings and we had lots of them. Every day almost in the summer months. If we were fishing, I was happy and so were the kids.

There were a lot of funny things that happened when we went fishing, but a couple stick in my mind. We were fishing in what was really a narrow, shallow ditch... the backwaters off the Illinois River. Bill and I were sitting on the bank waiting for a nibble and Todd and Troy were on the opposite bank looking for the ever elusive big one, that usually got away. They had a stringer with them that already had several fish on it. Suddenly they caught a fish. A good sized one, but not a trophy winning one, even though they thought so. They had learned very young to take their fish off the hook and put it either in the basket or on the stringer. They put that fish on the stringer and gave it a toss back into the water and suddenly realized the stringer was NOT secured. They had just thrown away their whole stringer of fish and I'm sure those fish were all swimming in unison , just like a water ballet to get away from those Patton boys who had by now thrown their bodies to the ground in sheer frustration.

27

Just that incident alone earned them both the title of Gilligan in my book. How I loved those funny times.

Another time Todd, Troy and I were all fishing during the day. We again were fishing in the back waters of the Illinois which back then was some of the best fishing in the area. We all stuck together that day and were sitting on the bank talking and waiting for a nibble on our line. Suddenly Troy got a bite. I mean that baby bent his fishing pole double! I said, "Holy cow Troy! That's gotta be a big one!" All three of us were excited and could hardly wait for him to reel it in to see what it was. He was reeling as fast as his skinny little arms could reel. As he got it closer to the bank, it raised it's humongous head from the water just long enough for us to get a peek at it. Oh my God that thing was huge and it was ugly! Scary, actually. Suddenly, snap went the line and the biggest fish we had ever seen was gone. Oh my sweet Troy was so upset. He just didn't know what to say or do. I think he would have jumped in after it, if I had let him. He had tears in his eyes as he just fell to the ground in disappointment that the fish got away. He wanted to show that fish to his dad that night. Finally I said, "Say shit Troy! It'll make you feel better!" He looked at me in disbelief to see if I was serious. I repeated it to him again. So, he sat up, hit his hand on the ground and yelled out, "SHIT!" Then all three of us burst into giggles and he did feel better. We spent the rest of the afternoon enjoying ourselves and reliving the big one that got away. I don't suggest that any of you give your seven year old permission to use that word, but it just seemed to be the only logical thing to say at that particular time.

Another funny time comes to mind when we were

fishing down by Chandlerville. We managed to find ourselves fishing in a body of water that was just full of baby, and I mean *tiny* baby bullheads. We would no sooner put our line in the water and there would be a two inch fish on the line. Talk about a pain. Bill was keeping so busy taking these tiny fish off the hooks and throwing them back in that he had resorted to saying, "Well, there's another one of them little bastards." Suddenly Troy got a fish on his line and he started getting so excited and he yelled out, "Dad, I caught a little bastard!" Little did we think that he was listening—never mind that he thought it was the name of the fish. Fishing with those kids was a riot!

I loved my children and I loved spending time with them. I think I was the only mom in all of Havana that felt sad when school started because I knew I would miss my children being around. If I had my way I would have kept them small forever. A big part of me didn't want them to ever grow up and leave home, while at the same time they were constantly becoming prepared for the day in their future that it would happen. They would be out on their own.

To lose a child was my worst fear as it is any mother's. I couldn't bear to ever let those horrible thoughts creep into my mind, but they still would get in sometimes late at night when I couldn't sleep. Sometimes in the way of a nightmare they'd get into my thoughts. One night I woke up screaming hysterically. I had just had a terrifying dream that Bill and the boys went fishing on the Illinois River and they drowned out there in that mucky water. There was no calming me down for a good half hour. Bill had to take me upstairs to see the boys for me to realize that it was just an unspeakable nightmare and that my sweet boys were tucked safely into their beds sleeping. That nightmare never totally left my mind.

One day I was reading an article in a magazine about parents who had lost a child. In this article it said that if a family loses a child, it seemed to be, most likely, the child that was the center of the family. That never left my mind!

Todd, Troy and Lori in 1972

CHAPTER

Troy, All Boy

I know this will be hard for any of you to believe, but our 'Little Blessing', Troy did have an ornery, all boy side to him. We always called him our 'Little Evel Knievel.' We still call him that when thinking back on different things.

There were some funny things he did and some that weren't so funny, but they were all a part of our Troy and who he was.

He was three years old when he got his first Big Wheel. For those of you who don't know what that is, it was a very low sitting, hard plastic, three wheeled vehicle that ran strictly on peddle power and the front wheel was much larger than the back two wheels, hence the name Big Wheel. Peddle power. Boy, did Troy have peddle power. How his little legs could go that fast we never knew, but I wish we could have had radar on him sometime just to see how fast he could make that thing go. That's when he became the first three year old stunt man. The first one in our family anyway. He would ride his Big Wheel up the hill to the neighbors corner which wasn't that far away and turn around and start peddling as fast as his little scrawny legs would peddle down that hill back towards our driveway. On the other side of our driveway there was a slight incline going into the neighbor's yard. As he approached our drive he would turn towards it and down over that incline, while simultaneously turning the Big Wheel on it's side causing him to go rolling head over heals down that hill and land sprawled in the yard with his arms and legs spread out, and there he would lay motionless. Cars would be coming down the street and see that boy go tumbling down that hill and lying there as if to be lifeless and they would stop their cars—just in time to see that little dare devil jump up and head back up the hill again.

Truthfully, right now we are on a search for a picture of our Troy on his Big Wheel. It's one of the most vivid pictures in our minds, but we can not find a photo of it and it's really eating away at us. Especially his dad. We all have a certain memory or picture of Troy in our minds that we hold dear. Mine is Troy sitting cuddled in my lap. I don't have a picture of that either. His dad's is Troy on his Big Wheel.

I just need to inject a little personal insight here, if you don't mind. Please, please never take anything for granted. Get pictures and get lots of them. You just never know what lies ahead and there may be a day that you will spend many hours crying over the picture you didn't get. The picture you wish you could hold in your hands and smile about or cry about for the bittersweet memories it holds.

When Troy was probably about one and a half to two years old, we got a puppy. It was a Beagle puppy and so gosh darn cute. I think we named it Sugar. Probably one of my sappy choices, I don't remember. I plead the fifth! Troy loved Sugar and Sugar loved Troy, but Lord I don't know why she loved that boy. He used to drag that little pup around like it was a stuffed animal. I never knew from one minute to the next what Troy would do with that puppy. One time I heard the pup making those little whimpering sounds like only a puppy can make, and I listened and followed the sound until I found her. She was in the clothes hamper in the bathroom. Gee, I wonder who put her in there? Another time I found her in an ice chest on the front porch. Once she visited the drawer in the buffet in the dining room. Troy never did anything really mean to poor Sugar, but I just think he wasn't quite old enough to understand that Sugar wasn't a stuffed teddy bear. He thought it was his personal life-like toy, just as he used to be Lori and Todd's life-like doll. Of course, they never put Troy in the clothes hamper. I don't think. *smile* Troy was always the one Sugar went running to. I think they would have grown up to be great buddies, but sadly our neighbor guy accidently ran over Sugar one Saturday afternoon. He felt so bad and of course we all cried as we had a little funeral for her in our back yard. Maybe it was God's way of keeping her from winding up in the hamper with the dirty socks. Oh gosh, I don't believe that for one minute. But, I do think Troy was much too young to appreciate the fact that a puppy was a living creature who needed to be treated with tender loving care. We didn't get another dog for years. And that one had an untimely death and sad ending too, although like with Sugar, it's death had nothing to do with Troy. Actually, when that dog got out the front door and took off Troy had went hunting for him and saw him lying in the street after it had been ran over by a car. A woman who lived nearby said that Troy kneeled there looking down at that dog with big tears falling from his blue eyes and sobbed, "That was my dog." She told me that story in the store while I was at work one day and I just broke down and cried my heart out. I couldn't stand for my Troy to hurt in any way and it broke my heart to know that his heart was broken. I promised him when he was born that I would protect him from hurt.

I know this probably all sounds like the rambling's

of a grieving mom, and I guess it is in a way... but, he was full of all the little boy antics that most boys are. Always pulling jokes on people and into something. I think I told you about the time he picked flowers from one neighbors' yard and tried to sell them to the other neighbor. I always told him he was going to be a banker or a crook when he grew up, because he was always coming up with ways to make money when he was only four and five years old. Then there came a time, when I worked at Pizza Hut that he would go with me when I did books at night, and he was always saying, "Mom, can I borrow a quarter?" Never did he say, "Can I have a quarter?" It was always 'borrow.' When he grew up I used to tell him he owed me over $10,000 in quarters from his childhood days.

He also was given the CB handle of *Window Breaker* when he was young, because he broke a window while standing on the console stereo. He was putting his butt in the window and trying to push the stereo out with his feet, to be able to reach a ball that had landed behind it. His guardian angels were with him that day, because he never got a scratch on his little, skinny butt. After he broke the window, he went running to the elderly gentleman next door, Adolph. He and Adolph were great buddies, and Troy pleaded with Adolph to save him and fix the window before his daddy got home. And Adolph being the kind person he was and loving Troy the way he did, came over and took the window and had the pane replaced and put back in before Troy's dad got home.

Even though Troy was four years younger than Todd, he always thought he could run and play with Todd and Lori and their friends out in the yard. And they did let him join in the hide 'n go seek, kick the can, and all the games they played on a warm summer's eve. Their friends thought Troy was funny, too. And he was. They liked teasing and horsing around with him just like everyone else did.

It was on one of those warm summer's eve that they were playing hide 'n go seek and Troy ran into a bush we had in the yard and it scratched his eye causing him a great deal of pain. If any of you have ever had an eye injury you know how much that had to hurt. I took him straight to ER, because you just don't take chances with an eye injury. The doctor gave me some salve like stuff in a small tube and told me to squeeze that into Troy's eye four times a day when I changed the dressing so it would not be irritated by light. About the fourth day of doing this I noticed something after taking the gauze off his eye. There was something dark colored in the inside corner of his eye, under the eyelid. I looked very close at it and thought it appeared to be something pretty solid— not just dirt or anything like that. I put my finger on the edge of the outside corner of his eye and began to rub very, very gently in a circular motion to see if it would bring whatever it was, out. It finally worked it's way out from under his eyelid and boy was I shocked! There had been a stick a quarter of an inch long (I know cause I measured it) under my poor baby's eyelid for four days! I was horrified and I was mad! I wanted to take that stick out there and poke it into that doctor's eye and tell him, "Now leave that in your eye, take two aspirin and call me in FOUR DAYS! That's how long you left that TREE in MY BABY'S EYE!" But, thanks to Bill I did calm down and didn't get arrested for assaulting a doctor. People just should not mess with a mom and her babies.

Troy had many experiences of being hurt, but always came out alright. I always said he had nine lives and I really believed that sometimes.

One day when Todd was in the back yard practicing his batting for baseball, there happened what could have been a real tragedy. Todd wasn't very old either. I'd say Troy was probably three, maybe four, so Todd would've been seven or eight years old. Todd was swinging his bat and just as he swung it, Troy walked right in it's path and it struck him on the side of his head. I heard Todd screaming and I looked out and saw him kneeling over Troy who was on the ground holding the side of his head, rolling around crying in pain. I saw the bat at the same time and my heart just fell out of my chest. I went running to the boys. I really don't know which one was crying the hardest. Troy because his ear had just taken the impact of a bat hitting him up along side his head? Or Todd, because he was the one swinging the bat? I know that I yelled at Todd for hitting Troy in the head with a bat and I regret that to this day. It was strictly one of those unavoidable accidents and if Troy had been hurt seriously, I just don't know how Todd would have handled it. As it was, I think the bat hitting Troy on his ear helped to save him from a much worse injury. His ear was black and blue for a long time, but there was no serious or long lasting injury done to him. God was with both of my babies on that day. I do believe that God has special Guardian Angels to watch over children and nothing will happen to them that isn't already written in their Life's Book. Todd was always the most gentle loving person you'd ever want to meet and as he grew into the man he is today. You couldn't ask for a man who loves more deeply than he. He loves God and he loves his family. I think Todd learned more from life's lessons than any of us did. He has grown into the man, husband, dad, son and brother that anyone would be proud to claim.

Todd and Lori spoke with a reporter shortly after our tragedy and one thing Todd said was this, "My brother wasn't afraid of much." Truer words were never spoken. I honestly don't think he was afraid of anything. Not even when he was small and certainly not when he was older and became a man. Troy was an adventurous man who took chances, that's for sure.

One time we had went fishing with a family who was good friends of ours. The kids were in the water playing to cool off and a snake came slithering across the water within reach of Troy. Not thinking for one second that he'd really do it, their oldest boy yelled, "Pick it up Troy!" As my little guy reached out to grab that snake just as he was told to do, everyone there started screaming, "NOOOOOO Troy, don't touch it!" He backed off, but he had no qualms of picking up any snake and wasn't old enough to know that some snakes can be dangerous.

He was riding on the shoulders of a neighbor one time from their house to ours. He was probably seven or eight years old, although he was small for his age. As the neighbor ducked down to come in our back door which was right at the top of our basement stairs, Troy just went leaping off his shoulders and unintentionally... I think... went tumbling down that stairway landing at the bottom. Scared the neighbor guy half to death. He screamed out and ran down the stairs expecting to find Troy with nothing less than a broken bone on his body somewhere.

By the time he got to Troy, he was already jumping up, a bit shaken but laughing at the wild trip he just took down the steps. He definitely had a Guardian Angel!

Troy also had a hard head... obviously. I don't mean that in the sense that he was a stubborn person. I mean his head had to be tough. While playing and running out in the yard one evening with the other kids in the neighborhood, we heard a loud noise that sounded like someone hitting metal with a sledgehammer. Nope, no sledgehammer. Just Troy running into the neighbor's lamp post and hitting smack dab in the middle of his forehead. Knocked him on his caboose. Even got a goose egg, but didn't break the skin or cause any other injury. His Grandpa Patton always called him affectionately, 'his little meat head'. I think it should have been 'hard head.'

One evening when Troy was ten years old he got out of the tub and came into the front room and said, "Mom, I only have one bulb."

"What do you mean, you only have one bulb?" I had no idea what he was talking about.

"You know? Down there" he said pointing down to his private parts.

Now, that was hard not to laugh at my son when I realized what he was talking about. I told him we'd go to the bedroom and check this out. And he was right! He had only ONE BULB! In medical terms that means testicle. *smiling again* That's my boy. Always the unexpected and always the funny guy, even when he wasn't trying. When I got him into the doctor they said that he could have been born that way, which was not possible because in ten years either myself or a doctor or Troy would have known it long ago. Or, it could have happened in a bicycle accident that pushed it up inside of him. How it happened wasn't really that important as either way it meant surgery to bring it down. It just about broke my heart to watch them wheel him into the operating room on that big ol' bed that made him look like a frail little three year old. I cried the whole time he was in surgery, but it all came out and DOWN just like it was suppose to. I firmly believe it was the latter of the two causes, since there was an accident that I didn't even know about yet and wouldn't know for several more years. He had hit a car while riding his bicycle one time and went flying into the air before landing on the pavement When I heard that story several years later, I said to him, "Well, that explains the mystery of the missing BULB!" His face turned red and he grinned. Oh that boy! Who's gonna tell me all the things I still don't know, now?

When our Troy grew up he still loved living on the edge.

One Sunday I got a call and he said, "Guess what I did Mom?"

"Lord only knows Troy. What did you do?" He had went bungee jumping. He said he almost peed his pants when he first jumped. haha That boy was determined to try everything.

Another day he called and told me that he had went sky diving the day before. Needless to say I was shocked. But part of me envied the adventurous part of his being—the part of him that made him not afraid to try new things.

41

At least one time I was upset with him over his latest adventure. Again, another phone call with the famous words, "Guess what I did Mom?" Actually, it still makes me smile to think of him calling with the stories of his latest adventure. Once again I said, "It's hard to tell what you did Troy. What was it?" He had jumped from the highest point of the Havana Bridge into the Illinois River. "Oh Dear God. Thank you for saving my son," was my first thought. My second thought was, "Troy, are you crazy or suicidal or what? What were you thinking? Don't you know you could have been killed doing that? There could have been a log floating down the river that you didn't see in the dark." He was like, "Well Mom, there were three of us. Another guy and a girl." Actually she was a grown up too. But, to me they were all kids. He told me the other guy jumped first and then the girl jumped. He said, "Once she jumped I couldn't be a wuss and not jump, so even though I was scared I had to jump." The bungee jumping and the sky diving were bad enough, but they were under somewhat controlled conditions. Jumping off the bridge was truly the Evel Knievel coming out in him. Evel Knievel with one too many beers in his system.

I've also learned that parasailing was one of his loves and that he did that on more than one occasion.

Yep, that was our Troy. He was always living on the edge and taking chances that many would be afraid to take. He just had no fear of dying or being hurt badly, I guess. I don't know if he had the idea that it couldn't happen to him or maybe it was something totally different. Maybe he felt he had something to prove to himself.

It was almost like our Troy had a sixth sense telling him that he may not have all the time in the world to do all the things he wanted to do. So he had to try them all while he could.

Troy, I wish you could call me now and say, "Mom, guess what I'm doing?" I know if there are any risks to be taken in Heaven you are leading the pack.

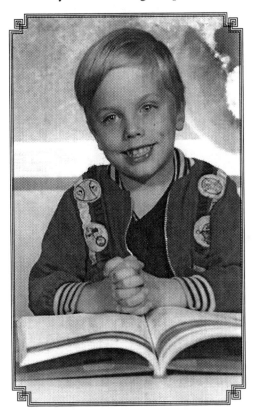

Troy in his little red baseball jacket

CHAPTER

Regrets — Part 1

4

If any of you watch *Ghost Whisperer* you know that Melinda Gordon (Jennifer Love Hewitt) communicates with earthbound spirits. At the beginning of each episode she says, "For me to tell you my story, I have to tell you theirs."

Keep that in mind, as this chapter will appear to be more about me, when in reality it is not. For me to tell you Troy's story, I have to tell you part of mine. Once a mother gives birth to a child, those lives are forever intertwined, and what one of them does will always have an affect on the other's life.

This will not be the hardest chapter to write. That will come later. But this is the one that I have to write in order to face up to the mistakes I made as the mother who loved her sweet boy so very much. The regrets I have deal with not always being the grown up, mature person I should have been. The things that make me cry now to think I might have failed him in so many ways. That sweet boy that I held in my arms and promised to keep from harm. Now I know that I caused some of that very pain I promised to protect him from. Actually, in all honestly I knew years ago that I had made the mistakes. It didn't take losing him to know that. It just took losing him to bring it to the surface again. Revealing my regrets will help you to understand my Troy and the things that made him who he was.

I don't know if I am the only mother who has made mistakes, but I feel like I am. It's hard for me to write about, so bare with me. Please. Troy did.

We had some really great times in our home while the kids were growing up. We really did! We laughed, we played jokes on each other, we did things together as a family all the time. Fishing, family cookouts and fish frys, ball games. Their dad and I both loved them so much and we never let them forget that I believe. There were always good times with our three children.

The bad times were between Bill and I and had nothing to do with our precious daughter and two sons. I don't even really know what happened to us. I think as we grew up (since we were only eighteen when we married) we just grew apart. It began to seem as if we had nothing in common anymore We fought. We fought a lot. We were under a financial strain after buying a home when Troy was six years old. That's when the money problems really started. Then Bill's place of employment went on strike and that just added more worries.

However, it didn't keep us from wanting to party on a Saturday night and bowling or dancing—even though more times than not it ended in a drunken argument. It had to be hard on all three of the kids. I know it was. Many times their dad would get angry and he'd say he was leaving and he would leave. I would end up being the one who told the kids that their dad was leaving because we just couldn't get along and he would always love them and see them a lot, but he wouldn't be living with us any longer. His leaving would ultimately turn into being gone Friday night, Saturday and Saturday night and coming back either Sunday night or Monday morning because he couldn't leave. It was because of the kids. That's why it was so hard. Every time I thought about breaking up my heart just broke because of the kids. How could they ever survive without their mom and dad together?

When I turned thirty I went through a couple surgeries which lead to depression and panic attacks. Once they got me on the right medications, I was on an even keel again, but their dad just couldn't understand it, as most people didn't thirty years ago. Many people still don't understand it. It caused a bigger strain between us and our relationship. Things deteriorated more each day. There were more times that he would leave and I'd think this is it, and the kids and I would once again go through the crying and the trying to make ourselves believe we'd be alright. And come Sunday night or early Monday morning he'd come home from a weekend of drinking with his buddies. I remember telling him more than once, "If you ever force me into being the one to leave, I won't be back."

Don't get me wrong. I am not blaming Bill. It was just as much my fault as his. We both made mistakes. Irreparable mistakes we felt. Things were said and done in anger by both of us that we just couldn't get past or take back. We tried on more than one occasion to move on and get things on track, but for whatever reasons we just couldn't do it. I felt that we were drowning in a pool of despair of our own doing and there was no good answer.

One Sunday night we had a particularly bad argument. I don't even remember now what it was all about, but I know that Bill left the house and I was pretty scared that he was going to do the unthinkable and I couldn't stand it. How would my children ever be able to live with that? Or me? If I was driving him to such desperate measures and making him so miserable, if he did come home safe... then I would leave. That seemed to be the only answer in my eyes. I called some friends and told them of my fear that night and I don't remember if they found him or he just came home, but he was okay. And I did thank God for keeping him safe.

The next morning I talked with the kids. All three of them. I was crying, but I told them that I felt like I needed to leave. That their dad and I could not get along and we needed to be apart and I didn't think he'd leave so I thought I should. I wanted their opinions. Lori was a senior, Todd a junior and Troy was thirteen. Lori and Todd were older and even though it hurt they both said they thought it would be better than us fighting all the time. I don't even know if they remember that conversation today. Anyway, the two oldest were saying, they agreed with me. I looked at my little guy and I asked, "Troy, what do you think?" And Troy being the same Troy he always was said in a very 'matter of fact' tone, "I feel the same way Lori and Todd feel." Oh my God, this is breaking my heart all over again to see it in writing after all these years.

Now, for the really tough part. I was working part time and only making $60 a week. I told the kids the hardest thing I ever had to tell them. " I'm going to our friends house (right here in town) and sleep upstairs in their spare room and every morning as soon as your dad leaves for work, I will be here and get you up for school and do the cleaning and the laundry and be with you as much as possible while your dad isn't here." It was killing me inside. I felt like I had failed all three of my children totally. It was the hardest thing I ever did in my life, but I left that day. I took only a few clothes with me. When Bill got home later I told him I was leaving and that I would come home each morning when he left, so I could get the kids off to school and clean house and do the laundry and whatever needed to be done. He seemed to agree with it at the time. Maybe because he didn't think I'd stay gone. And you will never in your life know how alone I felt each night when I lay down on that sofa upstairs and tried to sleep, knowing my babies were across town in their own beds. I felt like a 'bag lady', living in the streets, and that's exactly what I was. But, I kept my promise to the kids and I came over every morning. On weekends if Bill was gone I came over. It was hard on all of us and I thought most days I would just die from the guilt and the pain and the loneliness I was feeling, but still felt I was making the right decision, for both Bill's sanity and mine.

Everything went along like that for a little while and suddenly Bill told me that I had to get my stuff out of HIS house. I went over there and he had taken all my clothes and thrown them in a pile in the front room. I had no choice but to just throw them in the trunk of the car because I had no place of my own—no closet to keep my clothes in. I had just been getting things as I needed them when I came each day and did laundry. I don't blame Bill for that either. He was hurting and angry and maybe he thought that would force me back home. I don't really know. From that day on, I had my clothes in the trunk of my car which made me feel more like a homeless person than ever. Oh God, how did I mess things up so badly? And the worst part of all is I left my kids when I left that house, along with all the furniture, dishes, linens... everything. I thought if I left Bill with the house and all it's contents and the kids, it would help to hold him together a little better. That didn't really work, but I still think he was better off that I left him. There was no way

I could get a place for me and all three kids to stay. Not on $60 a week. But, I did see them every day. I couldn't even expect Lori and Todd to leave their home at that late stage in their lives. I believe it was March when we split up and Lori graduated the end of May. Todd had one year of school left and then he went into the Navy. The split up was not easy on any of us. I think Todd showed the hurt more than the other two. Troy felt it, but as usual kept things inside and pretended that he was in this perfect little world, hiding his feelings. One day after the break up I was working at the store in the Deli. I looked up from what I was doing and saw my Troy coming down the aisle towards me. He had one of his friends with him. He was thirteen, but looked so small and I saw his little face, and I could see in his beautiful blue eyes the sadness that lived within his heart and I broke down and cried my heart out. They actually had to let me leave work, because I just couldn't stop crying. Right now, I can see my little guy walking down that aisle and the tears just instantly spill from my heart to my eyes and run over onto the desk in front of me. I loved him so much, and my intention was never to cause him any sadness or pain.

In a very, very short time Bill went ahead with the divorce. His friends at his work place told him to get my name off his checking and not to let me in the house without him there. They were telling him that I would take his money and clean the house out while he was at work if he continued to let me come there each day. They didn't know me very well. Actually, they didn't know me at all. They just assumed I'd try to write checks on my children's father's bank account. A part of me still loved him and I knew there would always be a place in my heart for him, if for no other reason than he gave me three of the most wonderful children any mom could ask for. How could I not feel something for their dad? I didn't want to destroy him. I thought I was saving him, by leaving.

He got a lawyer, I didn't. He brought me a paper and told me to write down what I wanted in the divorce. It was a short list. My clothes and any personal gifts the kids had given to me. That was it! I didn't want any other material things or money—nothing from Bill and nothing from the house but my personal items. I'm sure his lawyer had to have been a bit surprised since we had been married nineteen years. Believe me, people were trying to get me to take Bill for a ride, but that was not my intention. I didn't hate Bill then, I never did hate him, I still don't hate him, and I didn't want to cause any more hurt than necessary, so I let him have it all. I am still thankful for that to this day. He's my kids daddy, why would I want to take him for anything? He'll always be their daddy. People that were suppose to be his friends said "Oh, you should take half his retirement." I said, "That will be HIS retirement. He worked for it. I didn't." I didn't feel I deserved a penny from him. I really didn't. I believe our divorce was signed by a judge on May 1st, 1984. I didn't go, since I wasn't asking for anything. Honestly, I'm not even sure what county it went through.

I was thirty-seven years old and out on my own for the first time in my life. I forgot to mention this earlier— Bill and I were married the day after my high school graduation. My parents were very strict and I went straight from them into a marriage. When I found myself on my own at thirty-seven years old with no dad and no husband to tell me what I could and couldn't do, I went a little bit crazy with my new found freedom. I was going out dancing on Saturday nights and I'd dance till the cows came home or they shut the lights out—whichever came first. I was quite the Saturday Night party girl. I don't think I sat out one dance. I'm not really proud of that now, but back then I was having fun and felt as if for the first time in my life, I didn't have a boss.

Unfortunately, or maybe fortunately, (whichever way you want to view it), my new-found freedom didn't last long. I left Bill in March and met a man the middle of May. He was a smooth talking romeo who said all the right things and made me feel more special than I had felt in years. Actually, we had both lived in the same town for years, but I don't remember having ever seen him. I soon found out that he had known who I was since my kids were small. He said he used to see me around town shopping and thought I was so pretty. As a matter of fact, once, years before, Troy had dropped my car keys down the vent on the dash of my car while I was in the parking lot at the grocery store. This dark haired guy had pulled in out of nowhere and stopped and asked if I needed help. I told him about the keys, and he rescued me by getting the keys out of the vent. I didn't know him then, and years later I didn't remember that it was him until he asked me if I recalled that incident. He said he told himself that day that I was one woman he would marry in a heart beat, three kids and all. I also found out that he was on the scene so fast because he had been following me when he saw me out and about with the kids. That should have creeped me out, but he was very good at sweeping me off my feet. With me being on my own for the first time in my life and without a place to really live other than that couch in an upstairs spare room. I was scared to death of what would happen to me. It didn't take much for him to talk me into moving in with him by the end of July or first part of August. I think I was going through a mid-life crisis at thirty-seven. Troy would come and see me quite often at the apartment. Then one day Bill came by and told me he wasn't going to let Troy come there to see me because we were living there and not married. I was devastated. So, August 13th, 1984 my Knight in 'not so shining armor' and I drove to Paducah Kentucky and were married. Now Bill had no reason to keep my son from me because I had a marriage license. It was all legal and I wasn't living in sin.

This guy had half ownership in a local bar here in town. It wasn't long after our marriage that he convinced me to give up that $60 a week part time grocery store job and work in the bar with him. So, that's what I did. I became a bartender and bar cleaner. That place needed some serious cleaning and I worked hard on it. I didn't realize that he really just wanted to know where I was at all times. That's why he wanted me to work beside him.

He was a restless type and the next thing I knew he was making plans to buy a bar in a very small town not far from Havana, and restore it. He and I would own and operate that bar on our own. He made it happen and it happened pretty quickly. We worked our fingers to the bone cleaning that place. It had been sitting empty for the longest time and we got a good business going there in no time. Troy came down there often, as it was only about ten miles from Havana.

Then, I think in less than three months after we

opened our bar, this man that I married said, "We're going to sell the bar and move to Tennessee. There's lots of construction work going on there and I'll be able to get a job easily." Oh my God! He's moving me away from my family? How could this be? I couldn't stop crying. I called my daughter and while hysterical told her what was going on. She told her dad and he was at the bar that night to make sure I was okay. I told him I was, but my heart was breaking. I wanted Troy to come with us, but I knew he wouldn't leave his school and his friends to live in Nashville and I didn't blame him. I asked him anyway, begged him actually. But how could I expect my baby to go away from his hometown? I never felt so miserable in my life as I did at that moment. God, this hurts to write about. This is all the things that I stuffed into the back of my mind and tried very hard not to let it come out—ever. Many, many people, before now at least, didn't even know about that second husband, because I was too ashamed to tell anyone.

I was secretly praying that we wouldn't get a buyer for the bar, but that was not the case. In no time the bar was sold and we were on our way to Nashville. I remember the day we arrived. It was a rainy, dreary, chilly day. We didn't even have a place to live. We stayed in a motel the first few nights. I felt so lonely and scared and homeless! We went apartment hunting and found one and paid six months rent in advance on it, rented furniture and had it delivered. When he decided we were moving from Illinois, we just moved. Took nothing but our clothes. God, what is happening in my world? It all happened so fast. Sometimes I wondered if he did that to me to get me away from my kids—but he did bring me home almost every weekend, only for me to cry all the way back to Tennessee. Every day I was there I hated it more and got more and more homesick. I spent every day writing to my kids especially Troy my sweet boy. I would sit on the bed and write and cry just like I'm doing now. I missed him so much and couldn't even imagine what he must think of me for leaving him like that. At the time I felt like I had no choice. I was married. Didn't I have to go where my husband went? By the time we had been in Tennessee for about five months, I just couldn't take it. I started making plans to take a taxi to the bus depot when my husband left for work and return to Illinois. I just couldn't live that far away from my kids, especially Troy who was by then fourteen years old. I don't know if somehow my husband figured out that I would probably be leaving or what, but he all of a sudden he told me to call Lori and ask her to find us an apartment here in Havana and we would be moving back. Oh Thank God! He was bringing me back to my kids. We were back in Illinois in February 1986.

We lived in Tennessee for almost a full six months, and I regret those six months more than any time or any thing in my life. If I had it to do over again, I would have said, "No, if you want to move, then you move. I'm not leaving my son and if you don't like it, tough!"

Dear God, I know I can't take it back, but please give me peace in my heart over that big mistake I made back then. A part of me never forgave that man for putting me in that situation to begin with. He knew my son was every thing to me. Why would he take me away like that? But a bigger part of me never forgave myself for that mistake. I should not have let anyone come between me and my baby and I have to live with that for the rest of my life. I did talk with Troy about that many times. He assured me that he was not permanently scarred from it or that he didn't hold anything against me. But I feel there was no excuse in this world for me to leave my son while I moved to a place so far away. A place I hated.

To make an already long story shorter, my second marriage ended in divorce in 1989. Did I mention that I was his fourth or fifth wife? That might give you some kind of clue how really stupid I was. But, I have to say that the woman he started cheating on me with, who was also married, did leave her husband and marry him and they are still married to this day. So maybe he finally found the woman he needed to keep him happy. I just want to thank her for getting me away from him, because my kids never did like him. I just didn't have the insight nor the brains they had when it came to him. Not for a while anyway. I think Troy liked him a little, but it was because he gave him beer to drink when he was visiting us. I didn't know that then. I always say that my wish is that if I live to be old enough, I will forget those five years I spent with that man. That to me was truly five years of my life just thrown away. At least in the nineteen years with Bill, we had three beautiful children to show for it. Bill and I have always said, "If nothing else, we did three things right in our life... Lori, Todd and Troy."

I remember the night that I drove through the Riverfront Park and there he was with the woman he was cheating on me with. I stopped the car, got out, told him and her both what I thought of them. Then I took my wedding band off and threw it as hard as I could into the Illinois River.

Years later that same scenario would be played out from the same spot, but totally different circumstances by a totally different person.

The Patton Family In Happy Times
Lola, Bill, Todd, Lori and Troy in 1978

CHAPTER

5

Regrets — Part 2

I find it very sad that there is a 'Regrets... Part 2'. If only we could turn back the calendar and relive our Troy's younger years. So many things would have been done differently if that were possible. There wouldn't have had to be any chapter in this book about mistakes or regrets. But nobody is perfect and maybe we were less perfect than some. I don't know. Whether positively or negatively, all these things had an impact on Troy's life and helped to form who he was.

Before even talking with Bill, I knew the very first regret he would think of.

When Troy was about four years old and Christmas was soon coming, Bill and a couple of our friends decided to go on a Saturday morning and cut down a tree for our home. Told Troy that they would be right back as soon as they found that perfect tree—and then we would put it up and decorate it, so Santa would be able to bring him his presents on Christmas Eve. They left probably around 9 a.m. and boy was Troy excited.

It's the little ones who make Christmas so much fun. Their bright smiles, the twinkle in their eyes, their anticipation of the gifts Santa will bring them. Oh how they try to be so good, because they don't want Santa to pass them by. The Magical Christmas Spirit was bubbling over in that child, and it couldn't help but to be contagious. I had the lights and ornaments all ready and sitting there waiting to adorn the tree with them

Troy didn't want to miss the tree getting there so he climbed into the window sill in the front room. There were three windows in a bay window type pattern, and they were long windows with wide window sills. The were just big enough for our little guy to crawl up on, pull his little legs up and sit there in Indian fashion waiting and watching for that big ol' tree that would be arriving any minute, because his daddy and his buddies told him it would.

The minutes were ticking by. Still no tree. Eventually, the minutes turned into an hour. I told him it would take them a while to find just the right one. After a while two hours had passed, then three. He still did not give up his seat in that window, and still had not lost his enthusiasm. I was able to convince him to leave the window long enough to eat his lunch and then right back there he headed. By now, several hours had passed and I knew... I knew that they were sitting in a bar somewhere or they would have been back long before that. I tried to get him to leave his perch and distract him, but he would not give up the vigil.

It was eight o'clock that night before they ever returned, and they were all drunk. I was so damn upset with them. I told them all, "Didn't you know this little guy would be sitting here waiting for his tree all day long? Do you know how pitiful it was to see him sitting there in that window waiting for his dad and you two to get here?" I was so angry I was shaking. Just to think they couldn't even go get one of their favorite 'little guys' in the whole world his Christmas Tree without getting sidetracked in a bar made me livid.

Bill just went to bed and passed out. He didn't listen to one thing I said. He was too drunk. The other two were drunk too, but the one guy did take the time to get that tree, which was beautiful by the way, set up for the kids and I to decorate. And when he left, with an apology to me and the kids, we proceeded to decorate our Christmas tree. I wasn't going to take that away from Troy or Lori and Todd.

By the time Bill had slept a couple hours or more and got up, we had the tree decorated. He was still drunk because he didn't sleep long enough to sleep it off. When he saw that tree lit up, he became so angry. He told me that I had to un-decorate that tree and he was going to throw it into the front yard because it wasn't right that we decorated that tree without him. Lucky for me and the kids another couple had came by to see us that night and were there when he got up. They were able to talk some sense into him and we left the tree as it was.

That was one of the worst memories and regrets that Bill would ever have and it still eats away at his heart. I wish he could let it go now, but I know just like me... the things we regret will always be in our hearts. Just as the love we had and still have for our sweet boy.

There were other things Bill would regret. He missed a lot of the kids life while out drinking with his friends. He regrets missing those Christmas programs his children were so proud to be in. He regrets the ball games he missed, although I don't think there were many of those. He regrets the Sunday afternoons he could have spent with his children, if he had not been sitting in a bar.

He missed lots of things because he worked nights part of our married life, so it wasn't his fault when he had to work the three to midnight shift.

It was the hardest for me when he worked the 11 p.m. to 7 a.m. shift When he would come home drunk in the mornings, there was no hiding it from the kids. When he was out at night, they most likely would be asleep when he came in.

You have to understand that Bill did not have a normal upbringing. His dad and mother divorced when he was about five years old and he never saw his dad again until he was seventeen years old. All those years he thought his dad didn't even try to see him—was not the case. His dad was also a drinker and that's why Bill's mother divorced him. She kept him from ever seeing the children again. He would come all the way from Pennsylvania to Illinois to see his six children and she would have them hidden at someone's house so he couldn't see them. He would send money, which she gave to the church and told the kids that he never sent them anything. Presents he sent, they never received. Bill was seventeen years old when he first found out the truth about his dad. And when Bill and I married we had contact with him and his new family and visited each other often. His dad was a recovering alcoholic and was sober for the entire time I knew him. So you see, it wasn't really Bill's fault. He didn't know what a normal family should be like. Additionally, I truly believe that alcoholism can be a hereditary thing. I'm not saying that Bill was an alcoholic, but he *did* let drinking come before many other things. Later in life, Troy would also let alcohol get in the way of the things that should have been more important.

Bill's dad and I talked in great depth on many occasions about his own alcoholism and he always felt so guilty for Bill and Troy's drinking. Even though I didn't drink as often—when I did drink, I drank to get drunk. If it didn't give me such horrendous hangovers maybe I would have never given alcohol up. I don't know. I'm glad I did quit, but I did my share of drinking in my younger life, too. I sure am not going to be the 'pot calling the kettle black', because I drank right along with the best of them at one time. I also partied with my youngest son before. We had a blast. So we thought, anyway. He was like me. He drank to have fun, and fun we did have.

There's one thing I'm certain of in this world. Our children never had any doubt that their dad loved them. They knew he did, and I knew he did. Hopefully, he knows in his heart that his kids never doubted his love for them and that they also loved him. Sure there were bad times, but when it came to our children there were more good times than bad.

One of the things that Bill and I both regretted even long ago was something that several of us were guilty of. We used to let Troy have sips of our beer or wine when he was just a little guy. We thought it was so cute and funny that he liked beer. One time a friend of ours put orange soda in a beer can and gave it to Troy. I don't know if he was even three years old yet, but he took one sip of that soda and he threw the can away. We thought that was hilarious that he could tell it wasn't beer and threw it away! Later in his life when drinking caused him problems, we regretted that we thought it was so cute to see him drink beer as a toddler. That is one of the things that I hope Troy has forgiven.

There was one thing that bothered me with Troy a lot and still does to this day. His dad and I talked about it a few days ago.

Troy was four years younger than Todd and five years

younger than Lori. Todd was very athletic and very good at basketball—terrific point guard. Lori was a straight 'A' student from the time she started school until the day she graduated. Bill and I did not compare Troy to his older brother and sister, but many people in town, including teachers, did. They used to say to him things like, "Are you going to be as smart as your sister?" or "Are you going to be as good at sports as Todd?" It was so very unfair of them to say that to Troy. I think too, it may be the reason he didn't go out for sports in elementary school.

We always felt that he was afraid of trying to live up to what people expected of him. It makes me cry now to think of that. He shouldn't have been put in the position of comparison to his older sister or brother. For that reason, I always felt he thought he was like the black sheep of the family, because he never went out for sports and he only got B's and mostly C's in school. But he was not the black sheep! He was a very important, special, irreplaceable part of our family, and we were very proud of him! I told his dad, that at least we can feel good knowing that we did NOT do anything to make him feel he had to live up to his brother and sister. And neither did Lori or Todd.

It's true he wasn't one of the best point guards to ever play basketball at Havana High, and he wasn't Valedictorian of his class. But he was loved by everyone who knew him—including those same people who when he was young put that pressure on his shoulders.

Lori and Todd don't have the regrets that we have. They were his siblings and experienced all the pain of divorce and the mistakes their dad and I made right along with Troy.

There is one time that comes to mind for Lori that she regretted so much. However, her and Troy came to an understanding about it before he left us.

It was Lori's little boy Tory's 3rd birthday party, in April 2005 on a Saturday afternoon. I believe we were suppose to be there at 3 p.m.. Everyone was there but Troy and his family. We waited for a while. Probably was a half hour or more before finally Lori got on the phone and called her little brother. She was already getting impatient as she said, "Hey, where are you? Don't you know that your nephew is sitting here waiting to open his presents and have his birthday cake?" For whatever reason, Troy immediately became defensive and went off on Lori. I didn't hear what he said to her, but I know he jumped all over her and she was pregnant with Taryn at the time, so her hormones were already raging. After she hung up from talking with Troy she said to her dad, "You call Troy and tell him I don't want him at my house. Tell him to just forget coming to Tory's birthday party if he can't be here on time and the way he talked to me, I don't want him here!" Oh my God. Here I go again. Tears on the pages. Her dad got on the phone and called Troy and said to him, "You better just stay away son, because Lori is really upset. It's best if you don't show up." I don't know what went through Troy's mind, because I wasn't talking on the phone to him so couldn't hear, but I do know he asked if it was alright to bring the kids over. His girls and his two stepchildren. Lori said they could come, but he was not welcome at her house. He came by and dropped the kids off along with the gift he had bought for Tory. How could Lori have known that it would be the last birthday of Tory's that Troy would be here for?

A few days after Troy's burial Lori told me that she had went to Pekin and on her way home she thought about that incident and she just sobbed her heart out all the way home. I told her not to let that eat at her, because they had come to an understanding before the unthinkable happened. Yet, when I got off the phone with her, I broke down and cried and cried. I was crying for the pain Lori was feeling, and wishing I could take it away.

This past April when we celebrated Tory's 4th birthday, I know it had to come into Lori's mind, because it was on my mind. I was crying inside for the party Troy missed the year before, and for the one he was missing now and for all the parties yet to come.

Todd had joined the Navy in 1985 and had made it his career. He retired as Senior Chief in November of 2005. That's when he and his family moved back to the area. For twenty years he was always stationed either in another state or on the other side of the world. There was no chance for him to have regrets, because he just wasn't around that much.

I have not seen many people with a faith as strong as Todd's. It's a beautiful thing to see, and he prayed about every decision he ever made in his life, both home and his career. He just knew God would lead him in the right direction and He did.

Todd did however, worry about his little brother and wanted to know in his heart that if the worst should ever happen, Troy would be welcomed into the Kingdom of Heaven. He wrote Troy a very long letter, which I never did see, but I did hear about it. He talked to Troy about

God and Salvation and what he needed to do to become a child of God and receive the gift of ever lasting life. Sadly, Troy did not acknowledge that letter to his brother. Todd's heart was burdened by that. It would be several years before that letter was ever heard of or talked about again.

Troy with Todd and Lori

CHAPTER

6

Regrets Or Adventures?

There were many things Troy did in his life that people, would surely think he regretted. I think he looked on them as the adventures of his life. To him they were probably right up there on his list with the bungee jumping and the sky diving.

The summer of 1986 when Troy was fifteen, he was taken to the police station for underage drinking. They didn't legally charge him, but they gave him a good talking to and scared him, I believe. The sad thing is, with Troy you just couldn't tell when something was getting through to him and when it wasn't. He was so good at hiding his feelings most of the time. He got that from his dad, because Lord knows I wear my feelings on my sleeve.

I picked him up at the station and took him home. I said, "Troy, why would you do something like this?" Didn't you know it was wrong?" He began to cry which wasn't like my Troy to cry over anything. He said, "Mom, when Todd left today to go back to the Navy I wanted to hug him goodbye, but I couldn't." Well, maybe he was playing me, I don't know, but it broke my heart instantly. I was already hurting over Todd being gone to the Navy and now my baby was saying he wanted to hug his brother and couldn't. Nothing in this world will get to a mom more than to think her babies are hurting. My heart just broke and the tears rolled. I said to Troy, "If you want to hug your big brother, then you hug him. I don't care if there is a thousand people looking at you. There is nothing wrong with you hugging your brother goodbye." We talked most of the night, and maybe part of it was a play on my sympathies, but I knew he was hurting too. How could he not. His mom and dad were divorced and he was going back and forth between my home and his dad's. His sister went out on her own and Todd joined the Navy—all in a little over a year. Don't even try and tell me my baby wasn't hurting, because I know he was. That is not even counting his mom going to Nashville, Tennessee for six months. Oh Dear Lord, how that boy's heart and mind had been messed with.

Nothing major really came out of that episode, because I got so wrapped up into his pain, that I kind of let the drinking thing slide, I guess. I know that was my fault, and it was wrong. I felt so guilty over everything that had happened in his young life.

The months passed and one day my daughter met a man. A man that we didn't really know because he wasn't from around here. He was from Florida and was a big shot engineer or something. They had brought him in here to revamp the power plant. He was dating Lori. He flew her to Florida for the weekend. He flew her to Michigan or somewhere for a ball game. He spoiled her buying things for her. They dated for some time and suddenly she told us she was moving to Florida. Oh my God! We didn't know hardly a thing about him, other than he seemed to have money and was smart. We were devastated and scared. Her dad and I decided that he should have the police run a background check on the guy, because we really were worried sick. I couldn't stop crying. How could my only daughter go away from us? She had a job with a lawyer's office here in town, had her own apartment and I thought was happy the way things were. She put in her two weeks notice on her job and told her landlord she would be moving out. I just couldn't stand it.

It was Troy's senior year and somehow none of us even thought about what it was doing to him. I guess he was usually so good at hiding his feelings that we sometimes neglected to think of his feelings. On the evening before Lori was suppose to leave, one of Troy's friends came to the door and he said, "Lola, you better come out here. Troy needs you." I was puzzled by that and wondered why Troy didn't just come inside. I walked outside and there was my sweet boy lying in a vacant lot across the street just screaming and crying out. I ran to him and he was so drunk. And he was hurt. He had cut his stomach on a broken beer bottle. He later said he did it himself, accidentally.

He was screaming and crying, "Mom, I need help. You have to help me. Please Mom, help me." I just felt such despair in the depths of my being to see my boy lying there like that. Between Scott and I, we got Troy into the house and Scott literally sat on him to keep him down. One minute Troy would cry out for help. The next he was screaming he wanted a beer. I called his dad and his sister. They were there within a few minutes. We had to find some place to take him. We called around and found out they had a place called Lifeway in a city not far from us. It was especially for teenagers who had drug or alcohol problems. They couldn't take him in for a couple of days, so we had him admitted to the hospital until they could get the room for him.

We also called Todd in the Navy and he flew in the next day. Even though Bill and I were divorced, we always were there for the kids as a family—still are to this day. We talked after we had Troy settled into the hospital where he'd be safe, and we realized that it was Lori leaving that had brought that all to a head right then, at that time. To Troy, Lori was the only one who had never left him and now she was leaving too. Oh how my heart broke to think of the pain in his young life. The sadness in his heart.

Lori did not go to Florida. It turned out that she was already having serious second thoughts and Troy being in trouble made her realize that she didn't want to leave. Troy spent thirty days in Lifeway with the other teens. Some with drinking problems, some used drugs, some both. He formed some close bonds while he was there in that short time, and it was very hard for him to leave there. He knew he was safe from the temptations as long as he was in there, I guess. When his thirty days were up, after a lot of hugs and tears with his counselors and fellow teens he left Lifeway and that part of his life behind.

I wish I could tell you that he never drank again, but that would be a lie. He started drinking within a couple weeks of leaving Lifeway. He didn't have a chance. All his friends drank. We would have had to take him away from this town to a perfect place where no one had any faults. I don't know of such a place. Do you? But, in spite of the heartbreak and worry, Lori did not go to Florida and she still resides in this town today and always.

If you ask me about those last two incidents with Troy, I think it might have been the two major things under his list of 'regrets', especially the last one. But, I can not be certain of that.

It wasn't too long after, that Troy's senior graduation came up. Every class to graduate out of this school had their parties and Troy's class was no exception. In fact, Troy was the party organizer for their senior party of drinking. They got busted before they even tapped the keg, I think. There were at least forty kids at that party and Troy is the only who was arrested and charged with underage drinking. He wasn't old enough to buy the keg and he couldn't have passed for thirteen never mind twenty-one, so I don't know why he was the only one who had to go to court. Maybe because they figured he was the ring leader. Anyway, he didn't go to court until after graduation. I had left my second husband quite a while before that. The judge sentenced Troy to one weekend in jail for that party, while everyone else just went on their merry way. I was not too happy. It's not that I didn't think he needed punished, I just couldn't understand why no one else got the same. He had to report to the Mason County Jail on a Friday evening at six and would be let out on Sunday evening at six. I spent almost the entire weekend crying to think of my baby in a jail cell. I was also scared to death that there would be a screw up and he would not be let out on Sunday. What a mom can't find to worry about, isn't worth finding.

After Troy's graduation, he and one of his friends were staying with me in the apartment I rented when my second marriage had broken up. He and his friends seemed to think it was party time every day. I was working two jobs and would come home from my part time day job, a program through the county, working for the elderly in their homes. I'd try to get a little snooze and then go to work bartending until closing time, 2 a.m. This was the same bar that my ex husband used to be half owner in when we first met and married. His ex partner was very good to me, and let me choose the hours I would work, and even let me have weekends off, always. I figured if I

79

was going to work two jobs, the least I deserved was the weekends off.

When I'd get home in the afternoons from my day job, there would be my Troy and his friends. Most days there would be a few other stragglers lying around on the floor watching TV and horsing around. This activity went on every single day. They would sometimes go work in the fields, but more times than not, they didn't even leave the apartment during the daylight hours because they had been out running around the night before. I knew Troy was taking advantage of me. I just couldn't get very angry with him because I harbored all these guilty feelings for the hurt I caused him in the past.

He and his friend would many times take the laundry to the coin wash for me. When I went to my sister's for the weekend, the apartment was always clean when I came home. If there had been a party, and I'm sure there were, they always cleaned the place up. Actually not long ago I got an e-mail from that friend and he told me that when they did have parties, Troy always made them help clean up before they could leave. He said, "Now, I call that love." I think it was more love than fear too, because I just didn't come down hard on Troy. Maybe he just didn't want me to be disappointed in him. I know if I could ask him right now, he'd have some clever answer with that little grin on his face. He was very quick witted which is why he had everyone around him smiling all the time. It was hard to get angry at him and even harder to stay angry.

Time kept marching on and I had met a very nice man, and we hit it off really well. So well that we were married sixteen years ago and still are together to this day. Problem was, he lived in San Jose and I was in Havana. I finally made the decision to be the one to make the move to San Jose. He, meaning my husband Larry, told me that Troy was welcome to come too, and I knew that. But I also knew that Troy would never leave Havana. I asked him anyway, knowing that he would go to live at his dad's. That was the best thing that could have ever happened. Him moving in with his dad. Because of that, he got off his little fanny and went out and found a job. He went to work for Pepsi in Havana on February 22, 1990. He went to work sweeping and cleaning the warehouse.

As it turned out, his career with Pepsi lasted sixteen years. He eventually decided that he wanted to become a driver, instead of working the warehouse. Frank, Troy's main boss at Pepsi, told us more about this after Troy passed.

The guy who did the hiring and moving people around at Pepsi had never let a warehouse worker move from the warehouse to driving. He just wouldn't do it, because he thought they were two different breeds of people. Troy was determined to make it happen for him, even though it had never been done before. He got the book and began to study for his CDL. Frank would take Troy down to the coal docks in town and let him practice driving the Pepsi truck. After Troy had taken the test and gotten his CDL, he put in for the driving job. The guy gave him the chance. As Frank put it, "Troy was like the pioneer that lead the way." Since Troy's accomplishment, in the years following, at least six others were able to go from the warehouse to driving. We had no idea that all this happened the way it did, and we were so proud when we heard that story. Not only that—all of Troy's customers on his route absolutely adored him as did his co-workers.

All this time, Troy did not give up his partying ways. He loved Nascar. One year, we believe it was 1992, Troy and about eight other guys, including Troy's brother-in-law and his brother-in-law's dad all went to the Indianapolis 500.

The story of what took place was told to me by Troy's buddy's wife and went as follows:

Scott and Troy were trying to go into a bar, but the bouncer wasn't going to let Troy in because he claimed Troy had already been in there that day and was kicked out. Scott was trying to tell the bouncer that Troy hadn't been in there earlier, because Troy had been passed out in the van. A cop came along and thought Scott was arguing with the bouncer so he ripped Scott off the steps and handcuffed him. This of course riled Scott and he was yelling at the cop asking what he did wrong. The cop said not to worry about it he was going to jail and began roughing Scott up (bouncing his head off the bumper of the squad car, trying to throw him in the car, etc). However Scott was too big and wouldn't fit in the back of the car because they had him hog tied so they had to get the cop van. All Troy did was walk up to the cop and ask how much it was going to cost to get his buddy out of jail. The cop looked at Troy and said "Don't worry about it... you're going with him!" Then he cuffed Troy, threw him in with Scott and off they went for a three day stay in Marion County Jail! There were hundreds of them in a tiny cell and Troy was scared to death. When his buddy's wife showed up the day they had to appear in front of the judge. Both of them walked out of the side door in jean shorts, no shirt, no shoes, and their hair was standing on ends. It was a sight she said she will never forget. They hit the first rest area so both of them could drench themselves with Scott's Brut deodorant. They smelled awful!

Now, I didn't know any of this until Monday morning, Memorial Day and it happened on Friday. It was pretty obvious why nobody wanted to tell me. I bawled all day long when I found out Troy had been sitting in jail all weekend. Because most everyone was from out of State that they locked up, there was no bailing them out. They had to spend the entire weekend in there and take their turn going before the judge on Tuesday, because Monday was a holiday. It was late afternoon before Troy and his buddy finally went before the judge. Stinky, looking a wreck, and a lot less money to their name after they paid the fine, but nonetheless, they were free at last. They both vowed that they would never go to another Indianapolis 500 — and they didn't.

Another thing that should be mentioned is that they got in line to use the phone over and over throughout their ordeal locked up. Each time they called my daughter and they had to call collect. She got a phone bill for over $300. You better believe that those young men had to pay those phone charges. I think they would have rather faced that judge again than to face Lori if they didn't come through with the phone bill money.

I don't want anyone to get the idea that I condoned Troy's drinking, but I have to tell the stories because they are all a part of who he was.

Troy's DUI. Scott and Troy (does anyone besides me
see a pattern here?), met up at a local bar one night. They
were both intoxicated when they left there, but neither
were ready to call it a night. You know... 'party till the
cows come home' mentality? They headed to a party
they heard was going on. Troy was driving his little grey
Escort north on Broadway. They reached a four way stop
intersection at the very same time a cop heading west
reached it. Scott told Troy to turn right and head east,
thinking the cop may not turn around and follow them.
Troy said, "Nooooo, I can't cause I'll hit him." I can just
see him saying that. So, he continued North on Broadway
and the cop turned and got in behind them. Scott told
Troy to turn into the drive of the house he and his wife
had just moved from not too long before that. Scott was
hoping if they did that, the cop would just go on by. No
such luck! The cop turned on his lights and pulled in
behind Troy. He came to the car and asked Troy if he had
been drinking. Troy said, "A little." This is when he asked
for Troy's license. Troy fumbled in his billfold and handed
the cop his FOID card. The cop said, "Well, that's a
form of ID, but I need your driver's license." Troy put
his FOID back in his wallet and started fumbling some
more and Scott saw that he was about to take his FOID
out again to give to the officer. Before Troy could do that,
Scott grabbed Troy's wallet and handed him Troy's driver's
license. The cop asked Troy, "So how much have you had
to drink?" Troy's reply was (as his head was reclined back
on the headrest and moving from side to side), "2, 12, 24...
something like that." Scott says he can still see Troy doing
that as if it were yesterday. The cop asked Troy to get out

of the car. At this time a lady cop pulled up. Scott had a talk with her and asked if she could help Troy out on this, because it could cause him to lose his job with Pepsi. She said Troy flunked every sobriety test, so her hands were tied. My sweet, but intoxicated boy got his first and only DUI. Fortunately, Troy had already proven to be such a good worker and everyone thought so highly of him, that Pepsi did not fire him. He had to pay a big fine, and could only drive if it pertained to getting to work, delivering Pepsi and driving home from work. I was very thankful that he had not been in an accident, and he did deserve the DUI.

It was during this time that he was at a party up on the north end of town. He was intoxicated and decided to walk home... even before the cows. He started walking. Finally, he reached his house. But, wait... he couldn't open the door. So he started beating on the door. At that time he was sharing rent and expenses with a couple of his friends, so they would surely let him in. An older guy opened the door and told Troy that he had the wrong house. Then the guy watched as Troy tried to get in the old guy's truck, thinking it was his truck. When he couldn't get in the truck, he just laid down on the ground and passed out right there in that old man's front yard. Someone called the cops and they showed up and took him to jail to sleep it off, but there were no charges brought against him. The next day he went to see, guess who... Scott. He told Scott the story of what happened and Scott, laughing said, "Well, you dumb SOB!" They talked and Troy felt so bad about it, because of it being an older man, that Scott told him if he could remember where the house was, he'd take him there so he could apologize to the guy. So, they went and talked to the old man who said he understood. He also told Troy he was not the one who called the cops and wasn't sure who did. They always figured it was a concerned neighbor who heard Troy banging on the door.

Things like that happened in this town on other occasions by other people. I once had an old guy trying to get in my door, because he was walking home intoxicated and thought it was his house.

Many of these things happened at a low point in Troy's life. He would never intentionally hurt anyone or even cause them fear or worry. But I also know that these things were all a part of life's adventures for our Troy. Our funny little guy that always spent so much of his life hiding his feelings behind those beautiful blue eyes.

Troy with Scott

CHAPTER

7

The Troy You Had To Love

After my last chapter about my son, I'm sure that many of you think he must have been known as the 'town drunk' or something similar to that. Let me assure you that was not the case.

People in this town loved my Troy and for very good reason. He was the kindest, sweetest, 'never hurt a soul' guy you'd ever want to meet. He was always there for his friends and they knew it and they loved him so much.

One woman told me that Troy called her on a Saturday morning and said, "I hear you need a dryer?" She said, "Yes, I do." It wasn't even an hour and Troy pulled up in front of her house with a dryer on his truck. He had her husband help him unload it, hooked it up for her and would not take a penny for it.

She said that if he ever came to their home and she was drinking Dasani bottled water (Coca Cola product), by the next day or so she would find a case of Aquafina bottled water (Pepsi product) sitting on her front porch. That was my Troy.

I remember one time he came by our place in San Jose that I happened to have Diet Coke in my fridge. He said, "Oh, yeah. See how you are? When I worked at Oney's Grocery, you bought groceries at IGA. I work for Pepsi and you buy Coke. Just go ahead and take food off your Granddaughter's table." Even though he was laughing, and at least partly joking, I felt pretty bad about that and I have always bought Pepsi products since. Even if Coke is on sale and cheaper. You hear that Troy?

This past September they had the Octoberfest here in town. We went down and met up with my daughter and her family. Larry went to get us a pork chop sandwich and I told him to get me a Diet Pepsi. He came back carrying a Diet Coke. He said, "I'm sorry, but they didn't have Pepsi."

When Lori sat down I said to her with a half smile, "Would you look at this?", holding my Coca Cola can up. "Is this sinful or what?"

She said, "I think Troy would understand. When I have both my kids in the van I go through McDonald's drive-thru and get my Diet Coke, because I don't have to get the kids out of the van and go into Circle K for Diet Pepsi."

I told her that I didn't think Troy would understand and he would probably have a bird poop on me or something if he saw me sitting there with Diet Coke in my hand. I know if he had been there, he definitely would have had something funny to say about me and my Diet Coke. I was sure I would, at the very least, spill it down my front or choke on it.

From childhood to adulthood, Troy was always the prankster. I remember one time I had fallen asleep on the sofa. Troy had been outside playing with the neighbor kids. Next thing I knew he was yelling at me like he was really freaking out, "Mom, wake up. Wake up! Look what I found on the street!" I woke up from a very sound sleep and he had his hands cupped right in front of my face, not six inches from my eyes, and there was a bloody finger resting there in his hands. I just went crazy and started screaming and jumped off the couch to get away from that gruesome find. I said, "Oh my God Troy! Where did you find that?" I was hysterical! My voice sounded like something straight from *The Exorcist*, I was so sickened by the sight of that severed finger. Then he and his friend bent over laughing so hard. It was HIS own finger with ketchup squirted around it. The little twerp.

When he was living in this house with some other guys sharing expenses, he took the toilet paper out of the bathroom and replaced it with a fake roll. When his buddy Rob went to the bathroom, he found out too late that the toilet paper was fake. He knew immediately that Troy was behind that stunt, so he had to think of a way to get back at him. So, each day he would go in and pour just a little water onto Troy's waterbed, to make him think his water mattress was leaking. The full affect of that payback would not be known for a few days.

Troy and his sister used to play pranks on each other all the time after they grew up. She came over one time with her husband and her dad while Troy was gone. They did all kinds of things to his house. Stuffed his mailbox with leaves. Saran wrapped his toilet. Put empty beer cans in the globes over his ceiling lights. Turned all the breakers off at the circuit box, cracker meal in his bed, switched his hot and cold water, stuffed paper towels in the sleeves of Troy's coat and then dumped ash trays in them, and even put salt in his ice water jug in the fridge. You name it and they did it.

What Lori, Troy W. and Troy's dad didn't know was that Rob had been pouring that water onto Troy's waterbed each day, so when they added the cracker meal to the mixture it was quite the mess! Troy got so frustrated that he took the sheets off and threw them in the garbage. When his dad found out about the prank Rob was pulling and how Troy threw his sheets away, he went out and bought Troy a new set of sheets. However, Troy still had to get back at them. They knew he would. They just didn't know when or how.

You would think Troy would have retaliated right away by doing something in return. But he was a clever guy. He let quite a bit of time pass. Enough time that I think his sister and her husband Troy had quit even thinking about what they had done to him. They had went somewhere and when they arrived home, they found all their wicker furniture from their front porch sitting on their roof! All the kitchen cabinet knobs had been taken off and put back on with the knobs on the inside of the doors and drawers. Light bulbs had been removed. Pictures were hanging upside down. He loosened the handle on the fridge door, so when Troy W. opened it the handle fell off. Anything he could think of to do, that didn't cause any permanent damage, he did to their house. He had waited a while, but he got them back.

Troy got his dad back too. He and some friends 'shrink wrapped' his dad's entire house and truck while he was sleeping one night. What he didn't think of, wasn't worth thinking of. He was always full of orneriness.

Troy's friend Scott told us about a time that Troy changed his voice and called the radio station to have them announce that there would be no school in Havana that day. They did announce it on the air, too. It didn't go too far though as the Superintendent heard it, and called the radio station to let them know that there would indeed be school. We don't think that they ever found out who did it. Yep, that was our Troy.

He used to borrow his dad's golf clubs and his dad

always told him NOT to leave them in the back of his truck! Troy always said he wouldn't. Well, one Sunday Troy borrowed his dad's clubs and the next day before Bill left town on his way to work he came by Troy's and there were the golf clubs in the back of Troy's truck. They had been there all night. So Bill just took them and put them in his trunk and didn't tell Troy. When Troy got up and found the golf clubs missing he was one nervous dude. He went crazy all day just thinking how he would tell his dad that the clubs were stolen, never mind how he would have the money to buy him new ones. Finally, later that evening his dad told him that he had the clubs. Poor Troy.

Another time his dad bought him some scratch off lottery tickets for his birthday. He was scratching them off and he got this look of disbelief on his face and he said, "Dad, you sure you want me to have this ticket?" Bill said, "yeah, why?" Troy said, "I JUST WON $10,000!" He was on the phone immediately calling his sister to tell her he just won $10,000 on a scratch off from his dad. Lori said, "Why doesn't Dad buy me scratch offs?" Then Bill's wife started reading the back of the ticket and found out it was a fake ticket. The kind that you can only claim at your Mama's House. It's only good if you believe in Santa Clause and so forth. Everyone got mad at Bill for doing that to Troy. Bill looked at Troy and said, "Troy, if you could, would you do that to your dad?" Troy said, "You damn right I would."

I myself felt sorry for my Troy when I heard about it. He was my baby, and I thought what a cruel thing to do to him. Then I went out and bought some of those tickets and did the same thing to my husband. What can I say?

Being a prankster runs in the family.

You already know that Troy was 'My Baby', because I've called him that so often. When Blake Shelton came out with the song, 'The Baby.' I listened to that song and the tears just rolled. I thought, just like millions of moms all over the country, that the song was written for me and my baby. While at Lori's for one of the grandchildren's birthday party, I told Troy that they came out with a country song about him and me. I started telling him all about the song and how it goes and by the time I got to the end where 'The Baby' didn't make it to his mom before she died, I was actually starting to cry, just talking about it. Troy immediately saw that I was getting a bit too emotional over a song, and he looked at me with those blue eyes (which I swear I detected a tear in) and said, "Why would I come rushing to your side?" Then he grinned that ornery, crooked smile and I began to laugh. I used to tell Troy that I thought he was put here on earth to keep my feet on the ground. He always had the knack of being able to lighten up any situation if the need arose. But, I always thought a part of that came from him always trying to hide his soft heart.

When Troy was six years old, (I spoke about this briefly in an earlier chapter), I had surgery. During the procedure my bladder was cut by accident. I was in the hospital for ten days due to that error. When I did get home it was on a weekend and I was doing really good. On Monday Bill went back to work and the kids had to go back to school. After they all had gone and I was home all alone, I was suddenly hit with what I would find out several months later was a panic attack. That one attack and not understanding what it was, sent me into a tail spin and I became very depressed for no apparent reason. I was afraid of staying alone. When school let out for the summer months, I was only digressing and had shown no improvement at all. I either couldn't sleep at all or I slept all the time. I cried constantly if I was awake, I couldn't eat. I was basically a mess and unable to function in the way I was always accustomed to. Todd and Lori were older and they would be off doing things with their friends and Troy and I would be home alone. He would come in and ask me if he could go down the street and play with his friend Chad. I always told him yes because I wanted him to be a little boy that didn't spend his time worrying about his mom. I would hear the back door open and close. Next thing I knew, there he'd be—peeking around the doorway at me in the front room to see if I was crying. If I had been crying, he would never have left me. That's how sweet he was at six years old. He didn't understand what was wrong with me, he just knew I needed someone and he wanted to help. Gosh, how that makes me weep now to think about it. He really was the sweetest little boy.

Since Troy's death I have had contact with many people that I did not know, but they knew him. They have told me stories of how Troy was always a friend to everyone. One person even told me that even though they had not ever had the chance to tell Troy, they wanted me to know that Troy had literally saved their life years ago. It was a person that he happened to run into at a local gas station. Somehow, he could tell that the person was hurting and hurting badly. He started talking to that person and they sat on the hood of the car and talked for a long time that warm summer's eve. Because of Troy taking the time to talk with that young person and boosting their self-esteem, it kept them from going through with their plan of ending their own life on that night. I promised that person that I would never reveal their name to anyone, so am keeping that promise... just as I know Troy would want me to honor that promise. I thought to myself, that even though I felt so guilty for the times he was afraid to leave me when he was just a small child... maybe that experience way back then is what made it possible for him to know when someone was in trouble. I'm convinced that my experience had helped to mold him in a positive way as he grew older. He had become the sweetest grown up boy.

Bill was always tougher on Troy than I was, even though many times he would feel bad later. He said that when Troy and Lisa were married they came over to his house and were showing off the tattoos they both had gotten done that day. Well, Bill was about half drunk and he got angry. He told them, "Here you two are without enough money to go around and you go off and spend money on something as stupid as tattoos!" Bill could be pretty intimidating when he was angry. Needless to say they didn't hang around long. I guess Bill forgot that he and I were even younger than Troy when we got married and weren't too responsible either. The next morning he woke up feeling pretty bad about jumping their butts like that, so he called Troy and asked if he wanted to go fishing. Well, of course Troy did. Fishing was in his blood. When they returned, they hadn't been fishing at all. They had both gone and got tattoos together and Bill paid for them! See? Bill was a softy too when it came to Troy. Especially, if he thought he had been unfair to Troy.

The day we put our sweet Troy to rest, we were all in our cars waiting to take the long, slow ride to the cemetery. Larry and I were in the same limousine as Troy's dad and Bernie. Everyone was just waiting and wondering what the hold up was. Finally, the guy from the funeral home came to the car and said, "There's going to be a delay. The lead car has a dead battery." All four of us simultaneously said, "That's our Troy." What good would it do, if it didn't affect everyone there? It had to be the LEAD CAR with the dead battery. On one of the saddest days of our lives, we couldn't help but to smile at Troy, our little prankster. He just had to get the last prank on us, and I know he was smiling.

Troy with his Dad, Bill

CHAPTER 8

Troy and Lisa - The Rocky Road They Traveled

Troy knew Lisa through school. This is a small town and everybody knows everybody, so it wasn't a surprise for them to start a high school romance. I guess it would have been in 1989, Lisa was a bit younger than Troy... about a year and a half, I think.

They made the cutest couple and she was a fun person to be around, the same as Troy. They had so much in common, and their romance blossomed. They went to the prom together and looked so cute all dressed up. They were a happy couple in high school.

Troy graduated the end of May, 1989. It was right after that he started staying with me in my apartment and he and Lisa definitely became a couple. I remember her coming over the Friday afternoon that Troy would be going to spend the weekend in jail for the graduation party he had orchestrated. That little stinker Lisa... she was telling Troy that she was going to be *this place and that place* over the weekend. I knew she was just being the immature teeny-bopper that all of us girls were at one time, and she wanted him to be jealous while he was a weekend jail bird. But, at the same time I was wishing she wouldn't give him things to worry about while he sat in jail. I honestly don't know if he worried about it or not, but being his mom, I was sure he would be absolutely miserable for that forty-eight hours. I know *I* was miserable. My baby in a jail was just the most horrible thing I could imagine.

In October of that year I moved to San Jose to be with Larry. Troy moved in with his dad and in February he had called and said he had something to tell Larry and I. By this time Troy had a small apartment in town. We came down to see him, and that's when we learned that he and Lisa were going to be parents. Oh wow! What mixed emotions that was for me. I really didn't even know what to say to him. I was hoping that they weren't thinking of an abortion, but at the same time I could only think how very young they were. The baby would be due in November of 1990. Troy would be nineteen years and eight months and Lisa would be barely seventeen. He told us that Lisa's mom was pretty upset by the whole thing and even threatened to have him arrested. Something else for me to worry about. Also, Lisa still had some credits to get before she could get her high school diploma, so her mom didn't want her to get married until she had her diploma in hand. She was worried that if Lisa got married first, she wouldn't finish high school. I couldn't blame her for that.

I don't even remember now, if I heard my daughter was expecting first, or Lisa. Didn't matter, both were having babies and having them close together. Lori's son Taylor was born on November 1st, 1990 and Britany came into this world six days later on November 7th. How cool was that to have my first two grandchildren that close together? And to have one grandson and one granddaughter. I was happy for all of them... and especially for me. I was a grandma twice!

I guess I should point out here that Todd and Nicki were married that summer on June 16th, 1990 and Larry and I were married on July 21st of the same summer. So, we had Lori and Lisa both pretty and pregnant at our weddings.

That year Todd and Nicki were home in November on leave. But, we all knew that he would be leaving before

Christmas to go to Desert Storm so he would only have a little time to enjoy his niece and nephew before leaving. I will never forget the last day he was home here in Havana. He picked up those little bundles of joy, one in each arm and walked away from us just looking at them and loving them and I'm sure praying that God would bring him home safely to them again. He was saying his good-byes to Taylor and Britany and I don't think there was a dry eye there, even though we couldn't hear his words.

On Christmas that year, we were all together. Except for Todd, of course. Nicki was here though and we had so much fun with those babies. We had little red and white long night gowns with the pointy caps to match and we were just posing them all over the place getting the best pictures of them. They weren't even old enough to know what it was all about, but the grown ups were sure enjoying it. Then we all unwrapped our gifts and I remember this so vividly. We were thinking of the pictures we wanted to send to Todd of our Christmas together. So, Troy being as ornery as they come and Nicki following right behind him for that title, both posed as if they were in this big old lip locking kiss, when in reality Troy had his hand between her lips and his. I can't look at that picture without smiling even now. And don't worry, Todd was able to see right away that it was done in good natured fun and that they were not really kissing.

As for me, I decorated my tree in red, white and blue that year and left it up until Todd came home at the end of May and we had his Christmas then.

Nicki and Lisa were both the sweetest and so much fun to spend time with. Still are today. They both have a wonderful sense of humor and fit into our family so well. That year while Todd was in Desert Storm, I don't know if they planned it or not, but Lisa and Nicki both made big picture albums for me. They had cloth covers and they said Cross on them. On the front of one of them they had put a picture of Todd in his uniform, holding those babies the last night he was home. Oh my gosh, I was just literally blubbering when I saw those albums. That was almost seventeen years ago and I still have both of those albums and they are full of pictures of the kids and grand kids. It brings back many memories for me to cherish.

That year Lisa completed her credits and received high school diploma. She and Troy planned their wedding for March 23, 1991. Britany was not quite five months old and wore a peach colored dress at the wedding just like the attendants and the flower girl.

My first thought was that Todd would not be here for his little brother's wedding and it made me cry to think he was in Iraq and Kuwait while Troy and Lisa were being married. But when I walked into the church that day, there was a table sat up with a picture of Todd, a candle burning and a yellow ribbon, since Todd couldn't be there. Well, those kids know they should warn me about those types of things, because I just cried my eyes out, it was so touching. But then again, I would have probably cried my eyes out, even if I had known it was going to be there.

Troy and Lisa were like looking at Barbie and Ken getting married. Except Lisa had dark hair. Troy looked so handsome in his white tux. All five foot seven and maybe one hundred thirty-five pounds of him, if you wet him down. Lisa was even shorter, about the size of a real Barbie doll, and a figure to go with it. Her gown was absolutely gorgeous and the two of them looked like something out of a fairy tale to me. Oh my baby was getting married, and he was still a baby, and so was Lisa. So very young for that kind of responsibility. But Bill and I were both eighteen when we got married. Of course, it didn't work out—but it took nineteen years before it didn't work. So I had every belief that Troy and Lisa could make a go of their marriage and love each other always. At their wedding reception that night, Troy was talking to me and he was looking across the room at Lisa, and he said, "Mom, I love Lisa so much. I think if it wasn't for her I'd be in prison or dead." God, how could I have known how true those words would be?

Any time I was around Lisa and Troy they were always laughing and joking. They were so cute together. Their personalities seemed to be matched perfectly and Troy had Lisa laughing so much of the time. I think that's important if your husband can make you laugh, and vice versa. They struggled financially, even though Troy had went to work for Pepsi in February of 1990. It's hard for a young couple starting out to make ends meet, especially when at times they just wanted to do something fun. Something off the wall like get tattoos, which I spoke of earlier. Or maybe they wanted a big fish tank about five foot long and two foot deep. I know what you are thinking. But when you are young and living out on your own, you just need something besides the stress of making ends meet. If you are even slightly immature, sometimes other things might take priority over the necessities, although they never would let the girls do without. I know there were very few times that Troy would stop in San Jose to ask if he could borrow twenty dollars for gas money for the rest of the week. Of course, I always let him have it and would tell him not to worry about paying it back. I'm sure Bill and Bernie and Lisa's mom and step-dad and her dad and step-mom helped them more than we ever knew too. I can't see anything wrong with that. There were many times in the young married life of Bill and I that we could sure have used a little help, because maybe we had spent some money foolishly. But there was nobody to help us. I guess that's why I didn't mind helping Troy and Lisa, even though it was very few times.

Watching Troy, Lisa and Britany together was just amazing. What an adorable family they had. It had to appear to other people that they were like little dolls playing house. But, they did love each other so very much. And in 1993 we found out they were going to have another baby. I was thrilled. I knew things weren't always perfect between them, but hey... who has a perfect marriage? And who doesn't struggle at times?

On April 1st of 1994, little Jessica Milyn was born. Oh my gosh, she was just as adorable as Britany. She had lighter colored eyes and lighter hair, but what a little doll baby she was. I always called her, and still do call her 'our little munchkin' because she is so tiny and petite.

Troy wasn't one of those daddies that worked his job and came home and expected Lisa to do it all. He pitched right in and helped with the house cleaning, the cooking, the dishes, feeding the babies, doing laundry, playing with the girls, and even changing diapers! He was a very good daddy and loved his three girls a lot.

Not too long ago Jessica was saying that she wished she was seven feet tall. I said, "Oh no, Jess! We love you just the way you are. And look at your mom. She's so small, I don't think you are going to get too tall." Jessica got that twinkle in her eye and she looked at me and with a great big smile on her face, she said, "And my dad! He wasn't very big either!" I didn't cry that day she said that, but I'm crying now. She was right. How could a mom and dad that were hardly any bigger than a bar of soap have a very tall little girl. She and Britany are both so beautiful, and that was no surprise. They had every chance of being beautiful, and they are.

Troy and Lisa's marriage was getting shakier each day. Although when we were around it didn't show. Lisa was always and still is a very loving person. She always hugged freely and was not stingy with the "I Love Yous" no matter which of us she was talking too. That's what I loved about her. She was just so easy to love, and we still love her.

I don't really know what broke their marriage, and even if I did I probably wouldn't tell it here. I only know that the day came in 1995 that they did break up their beautiful little family. My heart was so saddened and I worried about Troy so very much. He loved Lisa and those girls, and I am certain Lisa loved him, but they just were too young and could not hold their marriage together. Eventually all the responsibility of raising a family at such a young age just tore at the core of their relationship. What once was laughter and smiles and good times, turned into arguments and quarreling. They just had too much stress and the bonds broke.

It was at that time in Troy's life that so many of those

things took place that I spoke of earlier. The excessive drinking, the DUI, the going to the wrong house because he was so intoxicated. He had a really hard time with the break up. He couldn't eat and lost weight. Lori would tell me of both the emotional and physical pain he was going through and I just wept at the thought of Lisa and him not being together and worried about Troy every day.

If there is one thing I want to say here it would be this.

Britany and Jessica, my beautiful granddaughters; don't you ever doubt for one minute that your mom and dad were very much in love and you both were born from that love. You all were at one time a very happy little family and both your mom and your dad loved you with their whole heart. You were their babies and nothing in this world could take that away. Their divorce had nothing to do with you two at all. They still loved you both so very much and that didn't change. Even though they divorced, they remained friends and that made it so much easier for all of us, but especially for the two precious human beings that were brought into this world from the love of Troy and Lisa.

Jessica, Troy and Britany in 1999

CHAPTER

9

The Beginning Of The End

While trying to piece this together, I'm had a hard time figuring out just when and how Troy met Janene. Part of the reason for that is the fact that she was still married when they first met. Troy didn't want his family to know he was seeing a married woman I guess, so we didn't know about the very beginning. I'm finding out that I didn't know a lot. Their first encounter was a brief one, and it was a few years later that their relationship would continue.

The first time Troy's best friend and his wife met her was at their home. Troy was there to see them and he called Janene and she met him there. At that time she was still living in Fulton County. They sat around and visited and had a couple beers. Janene only had three or four and at ten o'clock she said she had to go!

Troy walked out with her to say their good-byes. Troy came back in and asked his friend to get a coat hanger because Janene had locked her keys in the car. They walked outside and Janene's demeanor had changed completely. She wanted her car unlocked and she wanted it unlocked NOW!

Scott went back in to get a hanger and in the mean time his wife came in and told him to hurry, because Janene was yelling at Troy. Janene had went into their garage and gotten the garden rake and was going to break the passenger side window out. Troy wouldn't let her do that, and she got irate with him. That is when they heard the yelling, and the next thing was the sound of glass breaking. Troy had broken her window out for her. They ran outside and asked Troy why he did that and he said, "She flipped out and made me bust the window." She left and the three of them went back inside. Troy told them at that time that he thought she acted kind of crazy and they agreed. It wasn't until a couple days later that Troy's friends found out she was married. That explained her big hurry to get home, and her insisting that Troy break her window so she could get in her car. Wonder what she told her husband about the broken window? Rumor had it that she told her husband she went shopping and her car was vandalized.

The first time we met her was here at the house we are living in. Troy was having a wiener roast for Britany's birthday. I didn't really think too much of her one way or the other, because she actually was pretty unfriendly and didn't have a lot to say. I guess at the time, I really didn't even think that Troy would wind up marrying her some day. I thought it was just another girlfriend he had met somewhere in a bar, even though you usually don't have a 'one night stand' come to meet your family for your daughter's birthday.

I do remember thinking, since I didn't know the story of the first encounter with Troy's best friend, that I would be glad if he had someone, because I knew he missed having a wife and a family life. The divorce between him and Lisa was very hard on him, and I shed many tears over the pain he went through, and I worried about him so much.

Eventually, Janene wound up moving to Havana to the housing project, and she and Troy had become a couple. But still the arguing went on all the time from what I have learned. She could be just fine one minute and the next just go off on Troy. Many times he didn't even know why.

He was still living in the project house and it wasn't big enough for her and her son and daughter. It's only two bedrooms. I'm sure it didn't take much talking for her to get Troy to buy a bigger and nicer house with three bedrooms. He had always thought he had to spend money on women and buy them expensive things. I don't know why he thought that way, because I certainly wasn't a materialistic woman who thought I had to have the biggest and best of everything. It's just that when he loved someone, there wasn't anything he wouldn't do for them.

It was October of 2003 that he bought the house on High Street for her and they moved in. The weekend they were moving in he had called and said that since Larry and I were coming down we should come by and see their new home. I said, "Okay, I'd love to see it. We'll be down before Taylor's birthday party." Not five minutes later he called and said it wasn't a good time to come down. I questioned, "Why Troy? If it's because you still have unpacked boxes sitting around, we don't care about that. We just want to see your home you bought." He explained that it was Janene. He said that they were hanging pictures on the walls and laughing and talking and suddenly she just went off on him and he had no idea why, and she had left! Larry was hearing our conversation and he said, "Tell Troy to tie another knot in it and hang on." Troy said, "I'm tired of trying to hang on." I told him not to worry about it and that we would see it another time. We came to Havana for the birthday party at the old gymnasium and Troy and Janene both showed up. You could tell things were tense between them, but at least they were there. They wound up asking us if we wanted to come by and see the house after the party, which we did.

Tears run freely when I think back to him buying that house for HER. He was so damn proud and couldn't wait for us to come see it. He was doing great, or so he thought. He bought her a big beautiful table and chairs for the kitchen. Actually, it was too big for that small kitchen area they had and should have been in the dining area where they had their TV and sofa and love seat. But, he was proud of the home he bought, and he worked at keeping the yard up nice and decorated for Christmas and Halloween. He had fish fries out in his two stall garage. Put a basketball hoop up for the kids. Had a place for pitching horse shoes. Sliding doors went out to a small deck where we spent many birthday parties visiting if the weather was nice. The house was so cute and I was happy for him, even though I always had worry nagging away at my heart.

Maybe it was because of Lori telling me what SHE was like... or maybe I would have seen it on my own, but I could see that he loved her so very much that there was nothing he wouldn't do for her. I didn't see her loving him back the same way. Unconditionally. I felt then and still do now, that she was using him. She had a daughter with her first husband and a son with her second husband. They were living at the housing and she wanted a house and she wanted it now. Of course, at that time Troy had perfect credit so he was able to buy her the home she wanted, even though he was already buying this house.

Their relationship continued to be rocky. I know because Lori would tell me. "Mom, Janene is a psycho and something terrible is going to happen some day." It always scared me half to death to hear Lori say that. I would tell her, "Lori, you're scaring me. What if she gets mad and picks up a knife and stabs Troy or something?" I even would comment that I hoped he didn't keep his guns loaded in the house. I knew Troy would never keep a loaded gun—especially with Jonathon around. He was just old enough that it would have piqued his curiosity if a gun were sitting loose in the house somewhere. Troy always kept his guns unloaded and locked up in his gun cabinet, and the shells locked up in the drawer on the gun cabinet. The keys were kept up on the very top of the cabinet inside a beer stein.

On January 31st, 2004 about 10 a.m. on a Saturday morning Troy called and asked what we were doing that night. I thought he was going to tell us one of the girls had a game or something. I told him we were doing nothing, and asked why. He said, "You want to come to a wedding?" "Who's wedding?" He said, "Janene and I are getting married tonight at the Methodist Church. I was shocked and thanked him for the eight to ten hours warning... with a chuckle and the thought, "That's my Troy—always the unexpected." He said Janene needed to be on his insurance because she was going to have to have a hysterectomy and she didn't have medical coverage, so they figured they better go ahead and get married right away. So, yes, he was my son, my baby, and even though in my heart I felt it might not be right for him, we came to their wedding that evening. He looked so very happy and so did she, but then she was the center of attention so why wouldn't she be happy? Part of me was so happy for him... but, there still was that worry nagging at my heart.

Not long after that we were back in Havana for Jonathon's birthday party at their home. Later that evening there was a surprise 70th birthday party going on at one of the local pubs for Tex, our close family friend. All of us would be attending that also. While sitting at Troy's that afternoon someone mentioned a woman from here in Havana... just in passing really. The second Janene heard that woman's name, who was at least my age if not older, she went totally off the wall. First time I had seen it happen. She started in on Troy yelling irrationally and talking so fast, you could barely keep up, "If she is at that party you better not even say hi to her, because if you do that's the same as a slap in my face! She's never treated me right and you better never speak to her!" She just kept it up, yelling and swearing like a drunken sailor. Troy didn't know exactly what to do, so being who he, was tried to make light of it. But his face was red and I know he felt so humiliated and at a loss as to what to say or do besides try to make funny comments. I felt sorry for my Troy and didn't know what to say either. It still breaks my heart to hear her talking to him like that. He didn't deserve that from her. I told my husband when we left there that I sure hope the woman didn't come to the party, because Troy would have hell to pay if she showed up. And why? Janene had no reason whatsoever to be jealous of that woman. Troy and Janene made a brief appearance that night, and the tension between them was so thick you could have cut it with a knife. The woman in question did not show. Thank the Lord.

For the next few months I continued to talk with Lori and would hear stories of how Troy and Janene were arguing and Lori always referred to Janene as her 'psycho sister in law', and it still always scared me. Any time we would be down here for birthday parties she never seemed to be smiling and happy like Troy and his family always had been. Troy was the one that was seeing to it that everyone had a glass of tea, cup of coffee, piece of cake and ice cream... not Janene. She was too busy nervously flitting around the house with an unhappy look on her face. It always made us feel we weren't really welcome there, as far as she was concerned.

It wasn't too long that we heard Janene and Troy were going to renew their wedding vows on July 10th, 2004 in Troy's dad and step-mom's back yard. I thought it kind of soon to be renewing their vows, but then found out that it was for the kids. Her two children and Troy's two daughters hadn't been there for the wedding in January, it all happened so fast. So this was to be sort of a uniting of the families. I thought that was kind of a nice gesture, really. At the same time, I thought... it's another way for her to be the center of attention. She was jealous of Troy's ex-wife and his girls. He told us on one occasion that she didn't like it that his girls slept in Brady's bedroom when they came over for their weekends with him. She told him that it was Brady's bedroom... not Britany and Jessica's. He felt so frustrated and asked her if he was suppose to make them sleep in sleeping bags on the floor in the living room.

Back to the renewal of the vows... Of course, we came down and there were so many people there! Troy had family that came from all across the country actually. He had uncles from the east coast, west coast and friends and family from several other states too. Todd even flew home from Iceland for the wedding. Troy was so happy that so many people showed up. And I made a point of saying to him, "Troy, look how many people have come here tonight for YOU. That's because they all love you so much that they traveled from everywhere to be here." He actually got a tear in his eye as he looked around at all his family and many friends who were there to celebrate such a happy occasion with him and Janene. On the other hand, there were only a very few people there from her side. Her immediate family, mom, dad and sister and I think one, maybe two girls she worked with came. Now, after all that has happened, I have to wonder if Troy was truly happy. After the ceremony (that Troy's uncle who is an ordained minister performed) there was dancing and celebration. We had what they call a 'Dollar Dance.' This is a custom that all the women pay a dollar to dance with the groom and the men pay a dollar to dance with the bride. As I sat and watched Janene I felt a sick feeling inside me. She was hanging on every guy that danced with her, grinding her hips against them and wiggling her behind. It was obvious that the guys were embarrassed that she was so blatantly being flirtacious with them. All these guys were there for Troy, because they loved him, and here is his new wife twisting and rubbing her body against them like the floozy she was. How very sad I felt to watch her making a spectacle of herself.

Time marched on and I continued to hear off and on about the arguing between Janene and Troy. His girls were getting to where they didn't even want to go to their dad's because they got tired of seeing her yelling and hitting on their dad, and him not doing anything about it. But, still I did not realize how very volatile the situation had become. I lived twenty-five miles away, so when I would be here I was an 'expected' visitor and things usually ran smoothly, even though she never seemed happy. She rarely ever smiled. She always acted like she was ready to go bouncing off the walls at any moment.

Janene always wanted to do their partying out of town, away from the people who knew Troy. She was known to start fights in the bars and of course then Troy would wind up involved because he was trying to save her butt. He got a black eye one time trying to break up a fight between her and another woman out in a parking lot at a bar. Then when everyone else went back inside or left, she just kept going in the bar and yelling vulgarities like, "Who the 'F' gave my husband a black eye? You just come out here and we'll fix you!" I was so afraid if she didn't hurt him bad, she would cause him to be hurt trying to protect her.

One time they had to go out to his girls' grandma's house to pick them up. He went in and she stayed in the car. She thought he was taking too long so she started laying on the horn. He and his girls came out and got in the car and she took off down that dark black top road driving way over the speed limit and smacking Troy in the face the whole time and screaming and cussing. She was in an out of control rage. His girls were terrified that they would have a wreck and be killed. They are lucky that didn't happen. That is a very narrow and dark country road. The girls went running into their mom's house crying when they arrived. And Troy, bless his heart... it's hard to tell what he went through the rest of the night with her.

They had traded Troy's truck in for a van and before

January of 2006, Janene had wrecked that van on three different occasions in a very short time span. Each time claiming she hit a deer. Actually, when the van and car were repossessed after Troy was murdered, the van was still crinkled all the way down the driver's side from front to tail end, because she claimed she had hit, yet another deer. They were being told that their insurance rates would go up after the second claim. Probably with this third time they would have had their insurance cancelled. Troy believed her when she said that all three times she hit a deer. The rest of us weren't so sure.

Troy had to live with her moods all the time, not knowing from one minute to the next what would set her off. Many times he didn't even know what it was. She'd just go off, as we all called it. But, for whatever reason, our happy, warm hearted Troy stayed with that woman.

One time the girls were at their dad's for the weekend and Janene 'went off' and went to the bathroom with a knife from the kitchen and locked herself in, threatening suicide. So, not just Troy lived it... my granddaughters and her two children did too. And always, and I do mean always, she got the attention she seemed to be starving for and my son would beg and plead for her not to do anything so tragic. She wanted him to worry and to beg her to live. She loved it. She had to always be the center of attention, even if it were just them and their children there. Actually, she had told people that she couldn't stand Troy's girls, even though she'd put on an act in front of all of us. It was because if they were around, she didn't get one hundred percent of Troy's attention. She had to share that spotlight, and that didn't set well with her. She didn't even want to share the spotlight with Troy. He was so caught in the middle of it all. My heart literally breaks to think of the stress he had to be living with, and yet anyone that saw him would have thought he didn't have a bad thing going on in his life at all. He was always the one bringing smiles to everyone else, when he so much needed to be the one with a happy heart. That's all any mom wants for her children... for them to be happy.

She was always telling Troy that her doctor thought she had cancer. I don't even think that was true. Nothing came of it, even after months went by. If she had cancer, or they even thought she might have it, wouldn't they have been doing something? And so Troy would worry about her health.

She told him and us, that the Lewistown cops harassed her because her ex was a cop there and she wouldn't put it past them to plant drugs in her car on one of the many times they supposedly would pull her over for no reason. We don't think that was true. She also told Troy that he should stay out of Fulton County, because he'd probably come up missing if her ex ever caught him in that county. Troy believed that too, and so did I and I was frightened for my son. Frightened that the police would do something horrible to him. She put that worry into my mind and into Troy's.

Many times Troy would be seen with black eyes, busted lips, or other scratches or marks on his face and he and Janene would both say that she did it and just laugh about it. Men don't like to admit they are abused.

She began to pull Troy away from his friends and family. Everything had to be about her and her family and friends. That's what abusers do, and he was letting her do it for whatever reason. If they did go out, it was always out of town. She didn't want him to run into his friends around town, because that would take attention away from her. She couldn't stand it that he was so well liked by everyone. She needed to always be at the center of attention. Always! I think some of the fights she got into at the bars was probably just another way of getting attention. She didn't like Lori either, because she knew Lori could see right through her.

I remember one time Troy called me and wanted me to look up Ephedrine on the computer. He said he was trying to tell Janene that she shouldn't be taking stuff with that in it. She hatefully yelled in the background, "Tell your mom NOT to worry about it." The only reason I even *knew* is because Troy, her husband, had just told me.

Troy did love her kids. Jonathon and him were great buddies. There wasn't anything Troy wouldn't have done for her children. He thought of them as his own. And her ex-husband that she told me was capable of doing something horrible to my son? He told us more then once that Troy was the best step dad to his son he could ever ask for. He said, "Jonathon loved Troy and I know Troy loved him too."

Did she take good care of their home? NO! When they were having company, Troy did the cleaning. We didn't see the bedroom areas, except that first weekend they moved in. After he was gone and we went there, we saw why they didn't invite people in that just stopped by. She was a rotten house keeper. Troy couldn't do it all. He put in long hours at Pepsi. I know he had to be embarrassed by the way the house looked. Why else would his brother be home from Iceland on leave, stop by Troy's three or four times and not once get invited into the house? They stood out in the drive way and visited. When Todd saw the house after everything happened, he knew why.

When he lived by himself after he and Lisa split up, he kept the house cleaner than most women would do. He couldn't stand to live in a messy house.

Her clothes were piled up in every corner of that bedroom! Her closets were full. She had more clothes, purses and shoes than a half dozen women combined. She was very materialistic and Troy bought her everything he could to keep her happy.

One Sunday afternoon in the summer of 2005, Troy and Janene went rafting down the Mackinaw River. That river looks tame enough to see it, but it is really a dangerous river with a wicked undercurrent.

It was a weekend that they didn't have the kids so they just wanted to get out and enjoy the sunny, warm afternoon. They were floating along with the current and suddenly they came upon a log jam that stretched the entire width of the river. The current was pulling at them, and they had to let go of the tube and were clinging to the logs to stay afloat. The current was so strong that it literally pulled Troy's shorts from him. They fought that current and were inching their way across the river trying to reach the banks. At one point they became so exhausted that Janene said, being the drama queen she was... "Let me go, Troy. Save yourself!" God, how I wish he had done just that. No, I don't and I am sorry for thinking that, but I can't help myself sometimes. He told her that he would not let her go and he didn't. After fighting for an hour they finally reached the banks and were totally exhausted and emotionally drained. Their truck was still a mile away, so they had that long walk ahead of them through the brambles and bushes. But at least they were alive. I know as sure as I know my name, that had Janene lost her grip and went under, Troy would have went under to save her and we would have lost them both that day. It just makes this grieving mom wonder why God saved them on that summer day just to have the unthinkable happen in January.

In November of 2005, Todd, Nicki and their boys finally moved back to the area after Todd retired as Senior Chief from the Navy. Gosh, it felt good to know my kids would all be in the same area for the first time in twenty years.

Larry and I were down here the first part of November for birthday parties again and Troy said to us, "Why don't you rent my other house from me, so you can be closer to everyone and it will help me out too, since my renter moved out?" We just kind of joked about it at the time, but when we left we got to talking about it and decided that maybe it was a good idea. That way when Todd and Nicki made the trip here from Metamora which was about an hours drive, everyone—including Nicki's parents would all be right here in Havana.

I called Troy and told him that we were thinking about renting his house. I think he was shocked but very happy. I told him we'd be down on that Friday evening to look at it again, because I hadn't seen it for quite some time. I said, "If I don't think I can feel happy living there, I won't move into it, Troy." He told me he wouldn't want me to move in if I didn't think I'd like it. The main thing I was concerned about was windows. I like windows where the light can come in, even though most days now, I don't even open my blinds.

When we came in I told him that I'd like for the rooms to be painted, but that I did like it and I thought I would be happy living here. He was so excited about getting it rented, especially since it was Larry and me. I sat down in the floor and wrote him a check right then, but we told him we wouldn't move in until Saturday, December 10th. We needed to give notice to our landlady in San Jose. We had rented from her for fourteen and a half years. Wow, was that an emotional experience for me. Larry had lived in San Jose since he was five years old and I had been there for sixteen years. I was so torn about whether it was the right decision and cried and cried worrying about it. I also was not up to getting everything done that needed to be done for us to move. All that packing and cleaning. Larry, bless his heart, let me hire a guy to come in and pack things up for me and also clean the carpets and floors once we were moved. That was such a big help. In the meantime we had a girl come to the house in Havana and clean just so we could move in.

December 10th, 2005. Todd, Nicki, Troy, Janene, Bill and his wife Bernie, and Larry's sister in law Jenny all came to help us move. Troy and Janene drove the U-Haul we had rented from Havana to San Jose that morning. We got to Havana in one trip. My daughter Lori and her husband Troy were here to help unload everything. We had made the move and once we got a lot of the unpacking done, I was so relieved. I was finally, after all those years going to be around my family and Todd was out of the

Navy. Everything seemed right in our world.

I had done our Christmas shopping before moving here and brought it down to Lori's and left it in her basement so we would have it here in town. Larry just had to bring it home for me to wrap. We had such a wonderful Christmas Eve at Lori's. Everyone seemed especially happy, because we knew that all of us would be closer and would have everyone together for every Christmas Eve from now on. I had gotten nice things for the kids and grand kids. I went out of my way to get Janene what she wanted for Christmas. One of them being a Nascar Kasey Kahne sweatshirt, because I wanted her to like it, so she wouldn't take it out on my son. Gosh, I felt so happy. My heart was more contented than it had been in years. All of my children together. Nothing could make this mom happier than having my three children together joking, laughing and horsing around They really knew how to have fun and enjoy each other. I waited so long for the day Todd would be out of the Navy.

Troy had went up to Todd's home in Metamora and helped him to move a big combination game table Todd got his boys for Christmas and they set it up and had a good evening together. They were looking forward to some fishing and hunting trips in the future. I was looking forward to some fishing too. Not that I had been invited yet, but I would have been, if I hinted enough.

January got here, and for the first time in a long, long time I didn't feel all depressed about it. It was the first part of the month and I found out that Lori's best friend was planning a surprise 40th birthday party for Lori. I decided to make her a slideshow going from the time she was born clear up until the present. I spent hours and hours in January working on that slideshow. It had seventy pictures and three songs and I was so proud of it. I stayed up all night, many nights, working on it, because it was just so important to me and it was what I call fun. I loved every minute I spent working on it and could hardly wait for everyone to see it for the first time at her party on February 4th.

We were hearing rumors that Janene was having an affair with a young psych patient at the nursing home where she worked. We also were hearing that the week of January 30th, 2006 she would be facing some kind of legal issues concerning her place of employment. But, that's all we knew them to be. Rumors. We figured that eventually the truth would come out, but little did we know how long that would be.

Around the time we were hearing all the rumors about Janene, she called me to let me know that they would be having Jonathon's birthday party on February 5th, the day after Lori's party. This was the week of January 23rd she called. While talking with her, she suddenly went totally hyper on me and began to talk a hundred miles an hour. She was asking me what she should do, because her best friend, who was also her boss at work had a boy friend who was cheating on her. Janene was asking me if she should tell this boss that her boyfriend was cheating? But, she never gave me a chance to answer and I didn't know what to tell her anyway. She just went on and on for at least a half hour about that woman and her cheating boyfriend. She said, "She's my best friend. Should I tell her? But, if I do tell her will she be mad at me? What do you think I should do? What would you do?" Personally,

I felt like for whatever reason, Janene was going off the deep end about it. But, later I would have to ask myself, "Was it really her boss's boyfriend she was talking about? Or was it the fact that her boss had confronted her about the affair SHE was having?"

One day, not long before the unthinkable happened, Troy's dad was in the grocery store when Troy came in. He said Troy walked right by him and didn't even notice his dad standing there. That was not like Troy at all, and Bill felt something must be wrong. He went to the back room where he knew Troy would be filling out the Pepsi order for the store and he said, "What's the matter son? Something wrong? You didn't even see your ol' dad." Bill said Troy looked up from what he was doing and he will never forget the look on Troy's face for as long as he lives. He said Troy just had this look like something terrible was wrong, but Troy being who he always was, answered, "There's nothing wrong. Everything's okay."

That look on our son's face still haunts his dad today and it does me too. Even though I didn't see it, just hearing about it breaks my heart and it makes me want to know what had our boy so worried. Had he found out everything was a mess with his finances? Had he heard the rumors about the affair? Did he know that something terrible was about to happen? Oh how we wish we could know what was lying so heavily on our sweet Troy's mind and burdening his heart. But we'll never know now, I guess. He can't tell us and it's for sure we could never believe anything she says.

On January 26th, I had Lori's slideshow finished and burned to several DVD's. I knew that besides Lori, her dad, Todd and Troy would all want their own copy of it. And of course me. Actually, Larry and I even went by Troy's house that night to take him a light bill that came here in Janene's name. It was a second final notice. Troy took one look at that bill and he said, "Well, there's a final notice on a bill we never got in the first place." Actually, we had already taken the final light bill from this house to Janene twice before that, but Troy was not home when we dropped it by and she obviously didn't tell Troy about it.

That was another thing. We had heard that Janene had asked the mail person to put their mail inside the garage, in the microwave stored in there, so Troy wouldn't get it. The mail employee supposedly told her no. Many days Janene would come home from her job in Lewistown on her lunch hour to get the mail before Troy could see it. It's because she wasn't paying the bills and he didn't know it. Or if she did pay, the checks bounced. The only thing that was paid up was his life insurance. Actually, she had written a check for it on January 27th, and that check bounced too. But since there was an eleven day grace period, Troy's life insurance was still in affect.

Back to the evening of January 26th. We pulled up in their drive and Troy came outside in his striped shorts, no shirt and no shoes and he was holding the little long-haired wiener dog he gave Janene for Christmas, Cinnamon. We talked for a short time and were on our way. How I would wish I had spent more time there that night. I live to regret that I didn't take him his copy of Lori's slideshow and leave it with him. How could I have known he would not see that slideshow? So many things we all wish we would have done differently.

On Friday night January 27th, 2006, Larry and I took the rent check for February over to Troy's house. I had put it in an envelope with Troy's name on it and a silly little smiley face drawn on it. Larry put it in the mail box and I called Troy's cell phone to tell him it was there. SHE answered the phone. She sounded irritated and unfriendly as usual. I told her about the rent. She said, "We are just leaving Kewanee and we are going to Lewistown tonight to visit friends" I assumed when she said, 'We', she was talking about her and Troy, but I wasn't certain of that. I wondered at the time how Troy happened to be in Kewanee already, when he would have worked that day. Little did I know how very much I would have been reliving that phone call and wishing that Troy would have answered the phone. I would have had one more chance to say, "I love you."

I had no idea that in twelve hours our lives would change forever.

CHAPTER

10

The Day Our Lives Changed Forever

The nightmare we were about to live, started with a phone call to Lori's home on that early morning. The following is her account of the beginning of that day, in her own words.

Lori: That Dreadful Call

It was our first winter in our new house. We had received our first heat bill about ten days before our first Christmas in our new house. Well, at least it was new to us. That first bill had us in shock for quite some time. It was astronomical. We immediately decided to make some temporary adjustments until we could come up with a permanent solution. Our last born, Taryn, was about six months old. Her crib was already in our bedroom. We had not moved her out of our room yet. You see, I always needed to wait for my babies to turn at least one year old before I quit worrying about sudden infant death syndrome. I always felt more at ease knowing that they were asleep in my room, right next to me. Plus, I was still nursing at the time. Our bedroom was plenty big enough for a crib. Anyway, after receiving that first heat bill, we decided to move Tory, our three year old son, into our bedroom too. His room, which would also be his sister's room eventually, seemed to be a lot colder than ours. We decided to keep our thermostat at a much lower temperature than we had before. Therefore, we needed to keep an electric heater in the bedroom in the evenings while we slept. Because we were all sleeping in the same room, except for my oldest son, we all were woken by that dreadful call.

That dreadful call came at exactly 3:36 a.m. on

Saturday, January 28th, 2006. The phone was on my side of the bed. I remember hearing the phone ring and instantly waking up and thinking... oh my God... why is my phone ringing at 3:36 a.m.? I am sure that most of you know how scary it is to wake in the middle of the night to a phone ringing. You automatically think the worst, which is exactly what went through my mind at that time. The first people that I think of when my phone rings in the middle of the night are my mom and dad or my mother in law. My phone has rung more than once in the middle of the night over the years and every time my heart seems to skip a beat. Most of the time it usually turned out to be a wrong number. I can only wish that the call I got that night was a wrong number. It wasn't!

I turned to look at the caller I.D. It was a cell phone number which does not come with a name. I did not recognize this number. It really scared me. My heart had already starting beating fast before I ever said hello. After saying hello, a male voice asked "Is Troy there?" I answered, "Yes, but he is asleep." The voice said "Lori, this is Mark" At first, I did not know who this was, but would figure it out real soon, or at least I thought I did. That part will come later. Anyway, he proceeded to tell me in a very mannerly way that there were a bunch of police cars and an ambulance out in front of my brother's house and that the street was blocked off. He said that something terrible seemed to be going on but that he wasn't sure what it was. The only Mark that I could think of was the one who lived right next door to my brother. I remember thinking that my brother and Janene must have gotten in another fight. I also remember thinking that I hope that she did not stab him. You see, I had always been fearful that she would do something horrible to my little brother. I always thought that she would stab him. I really cannot pin point the exact reason why I thought that, other than it just seemed to be her personality. Have you ever heard of a woman's intuition? Well, I think I had a severe case of it when it came to Janene. I had her number from day one.

Anyway, I told Mark to walk over there to see if he could find anything else out and to call me back. At this point, I was very worried, but I was trying to remain calm, thinking that it was probably just Janene being over dramatic like always. I had convinced myself that they had probably just been out drinking that night and that they had come home drunk and gotten into a fight. Even though I had always feared the worst and had told my mom and my friends of my fears, I just was not quite ready to accept the worst. My husband woke up to all of the commotion. I was telling him all about the phone call I just received. We were discussing what I should do. Should I go down to his house, should I wait to hear what is happening? You see, my brother only lived up the hill one block, down the hill one block and over one block. He was not far away at all. I am surprised that I did not hear any sirens. Although, I don't know whether there were any sirens or not that night.

And then, my phone rang again. It was Mark again. He seemed to be crying. He was very upset and almost hysterical. He said that she had shot my brother. WHAT!? I just could not believe what I had just heard. The guy on the other end of the phone kept saying to me that Troy did not deserve this. He did not deserve this. He did not deserve this. He just kept repeating himself. By this

135

time, I was becoming hysterical too. I remember saying "Oh my God, Oh my God" several times. By this time, I was pacing back and forth and back and forth. I can not tell you how many times I said "Oh my God" and how many times I paced back and forth in my bedroom. It was way too many times to count. I remember dropping to my knees more than once, thinking what am I going to do. How will I ever tell my mom and dad? I was already starting to go into shock, I think. My husband, Troy, was up, trying to calm me down. Then my two youngest children were starting to wake up. Remember, they were in the same bedroom. Tory was in bed with us and Taryn was in her crib about four feet away from us. I did not want them to wake up and hear what was going on, but I just could not stop the emotions. My oldest son was down the hallway and did not hear a thing.

I remember debating on whether to put my clothes on or just drive down there in my pajamas. Even though, I feared the worst, I was still hoping for the best. So, I thought that I could just hurry up and get there in my pajamas and find out that everything was O.K. and come right back home.

In the middle of trying to make that decision, I decided to call my brother's house. I don't know what made me think of doing that, but I did. I think that I was just hoping that he would answer. Instead, a police officer answered! Oh my God, I can't put into words what that did to me. It was the scariest thing. Then it got worse. I still to this day, do not know which police officer answered the phone. I know a lot of them, but not all of them. So I couldn't tell you whether it was anyone I knew or not. I told him who I was and that I wanted to know if my brother was alright. I remember that he put the phone off to the side, but I could still hear him. He said "This is Troy's sister." That was all I heard him say. I could not hear anyone else's response to that. But, after a few seconds, I was told that they were still trying to sort things out. I remember begging them to tell me something. They would not. Now that I think back on that phone call, I think that they already thought that he was dead or that they knew that he would never survive. His wound was just too horrific. They just did not want to be the one to tell me the horrific news.

As if I wasn't freaking out enough by now, I was becoming even more hysterical. By this time, both of my youngest children were up and crying. My husband was trying his best to calm me and them. He did not want me to go there by myself, but he knew I would and that I had to. I think that I was already beginning a total state of shock. Thank God, because I don't know how else I could have made it through that whole night.

I did decide to put my clothes on. I was planning to drive down there, but I remember Troy asking me to walk there. I think that he thought I was too hysterical to drive. Of course, I did what I wanted to do. I drove. Much to my amazement, I got up the hill and then immediately saw a police car at the bottom of the hill. I got to him and saw that there was no way that I was going to be able to drive right up to my brother's house. The whole street was blocked off from both ends. There seemed to be police lights everywhere. I began to think the absolute worst. I parked my van and walked a very fast walk to my brother's house. I wanted to run, but just could not bring myself to do it. I was afraid to get there.

As soon as I approached the front of the house a police officer met me there. They were watching me. They saw me coming. I knew him. I knew him well. He would not let me go any farther. He would not let me go up to the house. I think that he radioed in at that time that I was there. It wasn't very long before another police officer, whom I also knew well, walked out in front to meet me. They were doing their very best to try to make me calm, but it just was not working; I was begging them to tell me what happened. They would not do it. I just could not believe that they would not tell me anything. They did end up telling me that Troy was still alive and that they had called in the Life Flight. However, they never did tell me the extent of his injuries. He had already been taken by ambulance to the hospital, which was only a few blocks away. They suggested that I get to hospital and told me that my step-mother was already there. I remember wondering how she found out so soon. But, then I never did give it a second thought until later at the hospital. They offered to give me a ride to the hospital. I declined. I ran back to my van and called my husband to let him know where I was going and what was going on. I really wanted him to be with me and he wanted to be with me, but he needed to be at home with our kids. Later his mom did come in to watch the kids.

I remember calling my mom from my cell phone on the way to the hospital. I also remember telling her that Janene had shot him, but I did not tell her that it was in the head. I still do not remember exactly when I found out that he was shot in the head; I believe that it was from the phone call that I received from Mark. By the way, I mentioned earlier that I thought that Mark, my brother's next door neighbor, was the one who called me. I found out later that weekend that it was not Mark. It was actually MARTIN. Can you see how I might screw that up at 3:36 in the morning? Martin lived a block away from my brother. He just happened to be up at that time with his sick daughter. He also knew my brother just as well as my brother's next door neighbor Mark did.

I arrived in the hospital parking lot being told where to park, because Life Flight was coming in. I just still could not believe what was happening. You only see those kinds of things in the movies. I parked and went inside the hospital. My step-mom was already in there. We both paced back and forth, back and forth. I tried to get someone to tell me something, but they would not. We tried to call my dad, who was out of state, but he was not answering his cell phone. I remember pacing and pacing and pacing. I remember repeatedly saying "Oh my God, Oh my God, Oh my God". I also remember repeatedly cursing her. I hate her. I hate her. I hate her. Along with a few other choice words that I better not put in print. I still hate her to this day. I hate what she did to my brother and I hate what she did to our entire family. She not only took away my little brother that night, she took away my mom and dad that night too. They will never be the same. Who could be?

It wasn't long after I arrived at the hospital that my mom and step-dad arrived.

Lola: The Nightmare Continues As I Received The Call

It was about 3:45 a.m. or maybe a bit later January 28th,

and the phone rang. I answered with the panic already building because I knew it was bad news for the phone to ring at that hour. I never in my worst nightmare expected to hear what my daughter Lori was screaming and crying into the phone, "Mom, you have to get to the hospital. Janene shot Troy!"

"Oh Dear God... NOOOOOOO!" I began to pray as I was throwing on my clothes and Larry was doing the same. I repeated over and over, "God please give me strength and take care of my baby!" All the way to the hospital I was repeating that prayer, because I just couldn't bear to lose my Troy. There just had to be some mistake. She shot my Troy? This just can't be happening! "God please give me strength and take care of my baby!"

When we got to the hospital the whole area was all roped off with the yellow police tape. We couldn't drive up to the ER entrance. About that time the nicest young man with a red bandana tied around his head came to our car and opened my door. He said, "You'll have to park here, because Life Flight is coming in." "Oh God, I'm Troy's mom. Are they Life-flighting my baby?" If they were Life-flighting him then at least he was alive. That was a good sign, wasn't it? I was thinking that out loud, I guess... because the nice young man, who's name was Chris answered. "I was the first one on the scene after he was shot and I resuscitated him at the house. He was breathing on his own when they brought him here by ambulance. I think it just grazed the side of his head."

"His head? Oh Dear God... my sweet Troy was shot in the head? Please God. Take care of my baby. We just can't lose our Troy."

Chris was talking to me while he had me by one arm and Larry had me by the other and we walked what seemed like a mile at the time, into the hospital. My daughter Lori and Troy's step-mom Bernie were the only two people around when we reached the door. Even Chris had disappeared. Lori said they hadn't heard anything or talked to anyone. We were all just numb and so scared for our Troy. Troy's dad Bill was out of State for his Aunt's Funeral in Michigan.

There were no doctors or nurses around where we were. We were just by ourselves. We walked the floors and waited and waited. The chopper had gotten there and we saw out the doors when they rushed inside with the gurney. They all went outside but me. I still waited staring through the double glass doors where I knew they had my precious baby working on him. All of a sudden there were a half dozen or more people standing out in the hallway with x-rays lit up on the wall. I was standing there looking that way, wishing that one of them would come and tell us something. It just didn't even register with me until a couple weeks later that it was x-rays of Troy's head they were looking at. One guy looked up and saw me through the doors. He slowly walked around the group of people and stood between me and the x-rays. I then walked outside with Lori. It wasn't long until they came out of the doors with my baby on a gurney headed for the Life Flight. They saw Lori and I and they stopped in the middle of the parking lot and asked if we wanted to see him before they took him. (Now I realize they only let us have those few moments because they knew he was dying). We went to him, and he was all strapped in on that thing with a blanket wrapped tightly around his whole body. On both sides of his head there was a brace like thing to hold his head still. It was very tight on both sides and all we could really see was his face with his beautiful blue eyes closed and looking swollen. I was afraid to touch him for fear of hurting him. He looked so very fragile. I said, "Troy I love you. We all love you. You have to fight to live, you hear.? Don't you give up. We love you!" Lori was saying the same things to him. He made some kind of small noises which I took as a sign of him trying to answer us. Then they whisked him off to the helicopter and we went back into the hospital. We still had not talked with a doctor at that point... and when we did, the news was the worst news possible.

I cannot even tell you what he looked like even though I was sitting there looking right at that doctor as he spoke. He told us point blank— "I see no way for your son to live." He made a circle with his hands simulating the size of the catastrophic wound he was telling us my precious baby had in his head. He said even if he did live, he would never be the Troy that we knew and loved. "Your lives have just changed forever on this night." were his words to us. I know he must have said more... but by then the shock had really set in and I was blocking out most of what happened. I did tell him that Troy tried to answer me on the gurney. He said it was not possible for him to try and say anything. He explained that the noises we heard was Troy trying to breathe. Oh my God! How can he say that to me? I still believe to this day that Troy tried to answer me and I can remember those noises and the way he looked on that gurney like it was this morning.

Sometime during all this Lori had called Todd and told him to go to St. Francis Hospital in Peoria and be there to meet Troy when they got there, which he did immediately. He lives up that way much closer to St. Francis.

Larry, Lori, her husband Troy and I all headed for the hour drive to the hospital in Peoria. On the way Lori said she had the weirdest feeling going through her. She said it felt like adrenalin or her blood was rushing through her body in waves and a numb tingly feeling and it was scaring her. I told her that I was having the exact same feeling and it was the shock that God puts us into so that we can withstand what we are going through. I firmly believe that without that state of shock our Merciful God put me in, I would not have been able to survive that day.

Lori got on her cell phone and called Todd who was at the hospital and asked him if they had gotten there with Troy. He said, "Yes." She asked, "Is he alive?" Todd asked Lori where I was. She said, "Mom and Larry are with us." Todd said, "Just get here Lori!" I didn't know all of that conversation until later, but Lori said she knew when Todd wouldn't answer her because I was with her and to just get there—she knew. We got to the hospital and it was a short walk from the parking area into the trauma center. I walked what seemed like very slowly because I didn't want to hear what I was dreading in my heart. I was still refusing to believe that my boy could be taken from us. There was a little room off to the right that we were lead into. It seemed to be already full of people. I vaguely remember wondering how so many people got there so fast. One of the guys was the Coroner, which I would find out too soon. As we went in, I remember seeing Lori just falling against Todd sobbing, and I don't even remember hearing the words, "He's gone." but I guess I did. I just turned and buried my head into Larry's chest and sobbed,

"Oh God please help me. My baby's gone. Why did you take my baby?" I just couldn't fathom my world without one of my beautiful babies.

How did this happen? It seemed that one minute everything was right with the world and two and half hours later one of my precious baby's was dead. My sweet Troy had been shot in the head and he was gone. I wished that God would have taken me instead.

I wanted to cry out and scream, but I couldn't. Nobody else was... so, I couldn't be the weak one. They don't know what it felt like to find out your son was dead. They were all hurting and in the worst pain of their lives, but he was MY SON! I carried him in my womb for nine months and was there when he took his first breath. Only a mother can know that feeling of joy at the birth of your baby. And now he left this world, and I wasn't there to hold him while he took his last breath. Oh dear Lord. I couldn't stand it, but I had to keep it inside, because nobody gave me permission to scream out. My sweet baby had made the transition all alone. I hope it was a peaceful one for him. I hope it was as beautiful as people say it is. Troy, I'm so sorry I wasn't there with you when you crossed over. You had to do it alone. How I wish I could have at least been holding you in my arms. I know dying is the one thing that you really do have to do alone... but, how I pray that you were not afraid. I didn't want you to ever be afraid and alone. I promised to protect you Troy and I couldn't keep that promise. I know you went into the arms of Jesus, but how I wish you could have left my arms straight to Jesus, so I'd know you were not alone. The only peace of mind I have is that Jesus had to be holding you in His arms as you made the transition. I have to believe that. I DO believe that.

At some point in that small room one guy introduced himself as the coroner and told us that Troy's death was being treated as a homicide. Oh my God. She murdered our Troy? I guess all I was really thinking about was losing my baby, not the fact that she had murdered him. Murdered him with a shotgun blast to the head. What an evil, wicked, cold blooded thing to do to someone who would never have hurt a soul.

The rest of that day was a blur. At some point we all returned to Havana. We went by the house... the 'House of Death' is how I think of it. There were cops there, but she had already been taken to the Mason County Jail and was being interrogated. Later that day she was charged with three counts of first degree murder. She murdered our Troy!

Troy's dad was still out of state and unable to drive, as anyone would have been. So, his wife and two of our friends headed out to meet up with him in Indiana where his cousin had driven him. It was a six hour drive for them to get there and a six hour drive back to Havana in the pouring down rain. I can't even imagine in my worst nightmare what that was like for Troy's dad. He said he is glad he wasn't here when it happened and I am grateful that he feels that way. It was still the longest day of his life, I believe—waiting to be reunited with his other two children and grandchildren. He looked like a broken man when he came through that door about 9 p.m. that Saturday night. My other two children were there to meet him and hold him as soon as he walked in the door.

Eventually, we all had to go back to our respective

145

homes and try to get some sleep. The next day we would be going to the funeral home to make arrangements.

Sunday, January 29, 2006... my birthday.

I spent it with Lori and Todd at the funeral home. I couldn't help but to think that a little over twenty-four hours ago, I had two sons and one daughter. In the second it took her to pull that trigger, I had two children. Bill and Bernie, Lori's husband Troy, my husband Larry and Todd's wife Nicki were also there. We had to go about picking out a casket. Our first question was, "Will we be able to have an open casket?" Proper question, since he was shot at close range with a shotgun. The funeral home director said it took his right ear off and exited at the base of his skull. So, "Yes, they could fix him for the viewing, but he would have to be lying with his left side to the outside." They only had two caskets that could be used that way. One made of wood with a beautiful grain , so that choice was easy. It was perfect for our Troy. We picked out the flowers we wanted for the spray, and I swear I can not remember those flowers today. How sad that I can't remember them. I didn't even know I couldn't remember what they looked like until right this very minute as I was typing. That makes me feel so bad. We also had to give them the information for the obituary, what we wanted on the pamphlets that would be passed out at the funeral, and the 'Thank You' notes. Those were easy too. We chose the picture of the ducks. This is duck country, and Troy loved the outdoors and hunting and fishing. We had the Twenty Third Psalm printed on the inside. The Reverend David Byrd would officiate. Pallbearers? Troy had so very many friends. We finally narrowed it down to six pallbearers and six honorary pallbearers: Rob C., Mike B., Mike K., Chris P., Tony J., Scott H., Roy P., Todd W., Steve W., Mike M., Darrin B., Kenny M. There were dozens more that would have been honored to carry our Troy to his final resting place.

We wanted to have some music. This was kind of weird, but on Wednesday, January 25th for some reason when Larry got home from work, he had CMT on. It was the first time since we had moved to this house in December that we had the television turned to the CMT channel. The video by Brooks and Dunn, *"Believe"* came on. I had not seen the video or even heard the song before that day. Larry said, "That's a good song." I sat down on the sofa to watch the video and as I listened, I was so moved by the words that tears began to fall. It wasn't because it made me so sad—it was because it was so inspiring. To me it was anyway. The belief in God is what brought me to tears. Little did I know that four days later, I would be saying I wanted that song played at my baby's funeral. We also had *"One More Day"* and *"In The Garden."* That song was played at my father's funeral, and it brings me to tears each time I hear it.

We decided that we would have our Troy buried in his Nascar shirt and jeans. That's the way he would have wanted it. And a cap. A Nascar cap. You never saw my Troy without a cap on his head. And more times than not it was either a Pepsi Cap or Nascar. We couldn't find his Nascar coat, we think he might have been wearing it that morning. So, a very good friend (the very same friend who had bought the little red baseball jacket for Troy when he was just three years old) and who was much bigger than

Troy volunteered to let us hang his Nascar coat next to the casket and then it would be placed beside my baby before he was taken to the cemetery. We also would have Pepsi things around. We would have pictures of him all around and the funeral home would make a slideshow of my baby to have playing on a TV as the visitors came through the line for the visitation. We had to pick out a burial spot at Laurel Hill and we all let his dad do that. We trusted him to pick out a good spot, and he did. I know that had to be a hard thing for him to do.

We also had to decide on the time and the dates. The next day the 30th is Todd's birthday. I said, "I will not have visitation for your brother on your birthday." That would have been too hard, not that our birthdays weren't impossible anyway, but you understand my thinking. So, we decided on Tuesday night visitation from four to eight, I believe the time was. The funeral would be on Wednesday, February 1st at 11 a.m.

All throughout Saturday and Sunday the very guys that would be pallbearers for our Troy were with us. To sit there and see those big guys with tears streaming down their faces as they talked of the good memories they had was so hard for us to see, but yet so wonderful at the same time. They all loved him so much.

January 30th, 2006... Todd's Birthday

Monday morning the 30th, Janene made her first court appearance. Lori, Todd and some of our other family and friends went to it. Bill, Bernie, Larry and I did not go. We could not bear to see her that soon, although I did have

Larry take me to the parking lot and I watched as they took her into the court house in shackles and chains and her lovely black and white striped jail wardrobe. I'm glad I didn't go in, because Lori said her heart was about to pound out of her chest. They were in a small court room around a table. Lori said she could have reached out and touched her, that's how close they were. I could never have handled that.

On Monday afternoon everyone was busy finding what they would wear for the visitation and funeral. At about four I believe it was, we went to the funeral home to privately see our Troy. How very hard that was to do. But, if you can say your child, your brother, your daddy looked good laying in his casket... then, "yes, they did a wonderful job and he looked just like my sweet baby lying there sleeping." We were so grateful for that, because we needed that much closure at least.

The only thing I noticed immediately was that they had left his gold wedding band on his finger. I said, "He's got his wedding band on. Take it off! He can't be buried with that!" The funeral director apologized, because we had made a point of telling him we didn't want him to be wearing that ring. Before the visitation on Tuesday evening, the ring had been removed and given to my daughter.

January 31st, 2006

This day would be the second worst day of our life. Saturday the 28th, still being the very worst.

I was taking tranquilizers during this whole time, even though I didn't tell anyone. I had swallowed down three of them even before I reached the Mason District Hospital on that early Saturday morning. Three more before we went on Monday afternoon to view him privately.

Tuesday evening the 31st (which would have been Troy and that murdering witch's second wedding anniversary) we were waiting to greet people at his visitation. I said a prayer to God before I even went there. I said, "God, you know that I am sedated to get me through this." I didn't want my kids to be ashamed of me since they both were being so strong. But I pleaded with God, "Please let me remember the people who come through and what they say. Don't let this night be a night that just vanishes from my memory once it is gone. Please God... do this for me. Help me to remember this night in memory of my baby." And God answered my prayer. I was standing there with probably 15 mg. of tranquilizer in me to keep me from just falling to the floor in my grief Thank You God! I did remember!

We stood in that line for about six hours as the people just kept coming. And they told us so many good things about our Troy. Dozens of them were co-workers from Pepsi. I don't know how many dozens were his customers who he dealt with on his route. And all the friends from right here in town that had known and loved Troy his entire life. It was an awesome thing to see. There were 983 people who came through that line and shook our hands and told us how Troy had touched their lives with his kindness, his wit, his humor. It seemed everyone loved our Troy... not just us. Hundreds of people knew how special he was. We were told by people that they could be in the worst mood ever, having a terrible day and when Troy came into their work place, he would have them smiling before he left. I knew he always made me smile, but even I was just overwhelmed at the outpouring for our sweet, sweet boy.

One little guy that lived in the neighborhood Troy lived in and used to shoot baskets with Troy out in the driveway, came through carrying one of those small Pepsi cans. He told my daughter that he used to tease Troy all the time and call him the Coke Man, because he knew Troy worked for Pepsi. So, his wish was to put that small can of Pepsi in Troy's casket. My tears are falling as I write this. Lori walked the little guy up to our dear Troy and he gently placed that can next to Troy's arm and it was buried with him. Oh my, how my heart bursts with pride, but yet is filled with so much pain at these memories.

A lady from one of the convenience stores in Fulton County came through and she took my hands and she said, "We all loved your son so much. We used to tell him we were going to lock him in the cooler and just keep him forever. That's how much we loved him."

Another lady said that she didn't know Troy, but her and her Grandson would always see Troy leaving one of the stores on his route and he would always honk at her grandson. It made her grandson's day to have that Pepsi man honking at him.

One person after another and one story after another. The Pepsi guys. What an amazing group of people they are. They were there for us from day one. The very day that Troy left this world they were there, with food, bottled water, pepsi and their sympathy, and most of all... the wonderful stories they told of our Troy. Oh how he was loved and admired. And you know what really made him special? He didn't even know he was loved so much and so well thought of. He was just going through his life being Troy and by doing so, he touched hundreds of lives and hearts. God Bless all those wonderful people who paid tribute to our Troy and shared their stories and their love with us

February 1st, 2006

This day would be the hardest. We would lay our sweet Troy to rest and never be able to lay eyes on him again. Not in this world, anyway.

Oh how our hearts were breaking. Just as the night before... the turn out for the funeral was phenomenal.

People were standing outside in the yard, because there was no room left inside. Reverend Dave did a marvelous job and then Frank, Troy's boss with Pepsi for his entire career got up and spoke also. He just couldn't say enough good things about our Troy and probably could have went on forever about him. The songs were beautiful and it all went by so quickly... too quickly I felt... because soon we would be heading to his resting place.

I don't remember sitting there looking at him a lot in the casket, and I wish I had. And maybe I did... I just don't know. I wanted to remember every little thing about him, but it's hard for me to remember him in his casket, because I couldn't bear to just keep looking at him lying there. Lori and Todd said the night before at his visitation it looked like his grin kept getting a bit bigger as more and more people came through the line. They know it didn't really... or did it? I don't know, because I just couldn't keep looking at him. It was hard enough as I watched people coming in I could see the slideshow of my baby on the TV screen and the pictures were so hard to look at right at that moment for me.

When the funeral was over and the people filed out, some came by the casket to say goodbye and some didn't. Grown men sobbed out in their grief at the loss of Troy. It was all so very touching and so very sad.

The twelve pallbearers had decided that since they all loved Troy equally, six of them would carry him from the funeral home to the hearse and the other six would carry him from the hearse to his grave.

The family had already said their final goodbye's and were standing outside the funeral home waiting for them to carry our Troy out. When everyone else had left and was outside, those twelve young men put a 'stick on' number eight on the end of our son's casket. Troy loved Earnhardt, and the number eight was a perfect final touch. Only Troy's buddies that he watched so many races with would think of that. We all thank them for loving our Troy.

Everyone was finally in their vehicles and waiting for the funeral procession to leave for the long slow and sad ride to the cemetery. A spotless and shiny Pepsi Truck would lead the procession. That's the way Troy would have wanted it, and that's the way we wanted it.

Soon the procession was on it's way and you could not even see the end of the line of cars there were so many. People were parking along the highway and walking the rest of the way, because there just wasn't enough room. I don't even remember a lot about that part of it. I know Pastor Dave spoke, but I was numb and just sick in my heart that Troy was about to buried six feet under.

The four of us had went back to the limousine and some people were lingering at the grave. One of which was Troy's brother Todd. Suddenly we heard the loudest shout we ever heard and we didn't know what was happening. Later we were to find out.

While Todd stood at his brother's grave, thoughts of the letter he had written so many years before was laying heavy on his heart, because Troy had not acknowledged that letter. A young Christian woman who was a friend to Troy walked up to Todd at that very moment. She said, "Todd, do you remember the letter you wrote to Troy so long ago about God and Salvation?" Todd answered her with tears in his eyes and worry burdening his heart. She continued, "I thought you'd like to know that Troy brought that letter to me and we read it together and I talked with him about it and God and on that day, Troy said he 'believed' and accepted God as his Savior." Todd just shouted out rejoicing and fell to his knees right there and gave thanks to God that this woman lifted the burden from his heart and he could rest easy knowing his little brother was in the arms of Jesus.

I still can not believe it happened most days. But, I haven't seen my son except in dreams, and there is a monument in the cemetery with his name and picture on it. The home he bought for her sits eerily empty and lifeless, looking as though it is also in mourning for the life that was taken from it.

I can not hide from the truth, as much as I'd like too. My sweet boy is gone from this earth, and the long road of grief we were all about to embark on would be harder than anything I could have imagined.

Troy's Home
It shows the candles we lit out in the yard at 3:30 a.m. on the one year anniversary of him being shot.

I visited your grave today
The rain was coming down
I listened to the rain drops
Falling softly to the ground

I visited your grave today
Memories lingering in my mind
My heart seems dark and cloudy
Without my ray of sunshine

I visited your grave today
Thinking about the day we met
When I held you in my arms
My baby boy I won't forget

I visited your grave today
Remembering you at three
How you used to tell me stories
While you cuddled up with me

I visited your grave today
I thought about you turning ten
Was it really all that long ago
Oh, to live those days again

I visited your grave today
I saw your teenage years
The memories are bittersweet
I don't try to stop the tears

I visited your grave today
You were a handsome groom
You said, "Mom, I love her so"
As you gazed across the room

I visited your grave today
My son... ... a Dad of two
What a happy man you were
How proud I was of you

I visited your grave today
Some things weren't meant to be
Your marriage had been broken
Your anguish hard to see

I visited your grave today
Your life was moving on
God is the only one who knew
How soon you would be gone

I visited your grave today
The rain was coming down
As I listened to my tear drops
Falling softly to the ground

Lola Cross
7-26-06

11

The After Shock

Before I even begin this chapter, let me make it clear that I am speaking from my point of view only. I'm certain that even though this is exactly how I felt at the time, my feelings had to be tainted by the grief in my heart over losing my son. Lori is my only daughter and I love her with my whole heart and it is not my intentions to hurt her in any way. I'm only telling these things as the way they were perceived by me, and that does not necessarily make them accurate in her point of view... only in mine. I love you Lori.

I suppose that many people who haven't traveled this road, think that once the burial on Wednesday was over, things would get easier. How I wish that were the case. But, we were about to learn that we had not even touched the surface of our grief and anger. And I certainly did not think for one second that my relationship with my daughter would almost be destroyed in the process.

Thursday morning I woke very early... still do most mornings. Before 5:36 a.m., the time he was pronounced dead. I lay there with tears silently falling to my pillow and watch the minutes tick away until it reaches that exact time... 5:36 a.m.. Then I continue to lay there and cry softly at the loss of my precious son. Some days, in the beginning, I would lay there like that for more than two hours. Eventually I would force myself to get up. I didn't want to get up. I didn't want to face a single day without my Troy.

I had asked Larry to please stay home with me for the next four days, Thursday, Friday, Saturday and Sunday because I just didn't want to be alone. We decided that even though we had just buried my son, we needed to

159

use those days to get some things taken care of in Pekin. We got our dog groomed and we needed to get our taxes done. I figured that since we were going, I needed to see my doctor. I had called her and told her that I had been taking more tranquilizers than prescribed and why I had been doing so. She had no idea that my son had been murdered and told me to come by her office and she would see me that morning.

When I went in there, I immediately broke into uncontrollable sobs. I cried and cried so hard, that I truly believe the sobs were coming from the very depths of my soul. The way I needed to cry throughout the whole five days prior. But I didn't allow myself to cry out in my pain, because everyone else was seemingly being so strong. My son had been murdered and my heart was shattered and I just felt like it was not alright to just scream and go crazy in my grief. I had been holding it in, trying to be strong like everyone else, when the whole time I felt like my mind was crumbling right along with my heart. Quite honestly I felt I would surely lose my mind totally by not letting my grief out. I felt I was on the outside of the whole thing looking in and it was the strangest feeling.

I remembered a couple of years before, I had met a woman in the doctor's office who had lost her child tragically. She was still carrying so much grief and anguish inside, and my heart broke for her. Never did I think I would be going through the same thing. But, here I was, the day after we buried my sweet baby, and told my doctor, "I don't know how I'm going to get through this. I really don't. But I do know I don't want to be still going insane two years later." Unfortunately, for a while I felt I was going completely insane.

We got through the weekend. On Saturday we went to Lori's and she said Jessica was going to dispose of her daddy's wedding band the funeral director had removed from his finger and given to Lori. My daughter wanted so very much to be the one to get rid of that ring, but she thought it more important that Jessica have the honors. Larry, Lori, Jessica and I all went down to the river. The exact same spot that I had thrown my wedding band from seventeen years ago. Jessica took that wedding band and threw it as hard as she could into that Illinois River. And then we all cheered that it was gone. It was like one door on our pain had been closed. But, dear God... it was like working our way through a maze... a maze built from our grief.

On Monday morning Larry went back to work. I woke early as I had been doing and laid there waiting for the clock to reach 5:36 a.m.. Those mornings were so very hard because each time I woke from my sleep, I had to face it all over again. The numbness that God had put me into was starting to lift a bit more each day, and as it did so... my pain became greater. I was beside myself with grief. I would get out of bed, but most days I didn't get dressed. I just sat here in the house alone. Didn't even turn the television on, which I had always done for years first thing in the morning. I sat here and I cried and I missed my son. I became angrier and angrier and more depressed with each passing day. Larry would come home from work, and I would be sitting. Not dressed, no television, no lights. I wasn't even getting on my computer.

That Friday Lori called and I was beside myself. I just started screaming into the phone, "I WANT HIM BACK AND I WANT HIM BACK NOW!" I just wanted to die with him, so I didn't have to feel the pain. Lori said, "What did you do today, Mom? Did you get dressed? Did you put your make-up on? Did you get out of the house?" I was livid! Did she think that me getting dressed and putting make-up on would take away my pain? She said, "At least Dad gets out and goes places!" I screamed at her, "Just because your dad goes to the VFW and drinks doesn't mean he's handling it any better than I am!" She yelled back at me and said, "Don't you dare talk about my Dad!" I was crying hysterically and handed the phone to Larry, because God help me, I couldn't understand at that time where her thinking was coming from. Troy had been gone thirteen days, and she was telling me to get dressed and put my make-up on like that would make everything alright. Actually, I had done that on more than one day. Got up and showered, got dressed, put make-up on, and went about cleaning house and the tears rolled the whole time I was keeping busy. I couldn't stand it that he was gone, and all the grief and tears I held in for those five days were coming back to haunt me now.

In the irrational thinking my grief was causing me, I was saying cruel and mean things to Lori about how I couldn't believe she was so cold and uncaring. I said, "You are a mother for God's sake. Seems like you of all people would have some idea of how it would feel to lose a child." We couldn't talk. We could only yell and hang up the phone on each other.

I was sitting there watching as her dad came in that dreadful Saturday night. She and Todd met their dad at the door and she hugged him and held him and wept. I was heartbroken for them all. They all loved Troy so much. Bill's loss was just as great as mine. He was like a broken man and I could definitely feel his pain. I knew how his heart was shattered, because mine was too. But, with God as my witness I could not then, and still do not now... remember Lori hugging me at any time that day. I know she did, because she has told me she did, but with the self sedating and the sheer trauma and shock of it all, I just can not remember it and it just crushed my very being to feel she was not there for me.

I also think there is a difference in hugging someone and holding someone. She actually 'held' her dad as they both wept in their united sorrow. And that is exactly what she should have done. 'Hold' him and weep with him.

Throughout the days following Troy's murder, many women enveloped me in their arms and held me so close and I knew they were literally trying to take some of the pain from my heart and put it into theirs so that I would be able to withstand it. I knew that and felt it, because I had did that very thing with my youngest sister when she lost her twenty-one year old son in a train/truck accident sixteen years prior to Troy's murder. I think only another mother can even remotely imagine the pain of losing a child and they will 'hold on' with all their might and try to drain some of the pain from the heart of that grieving mom. They truly want to help by sharing that grief the only way they know how. By holding that mom and weeping with her.

I didn't get to experience that same sharing of grief with my daughter, and that's what hurt so deeply.

The hours kept passing as did the days and my emotions were like riding a roller coaster. I continued to try and hide my pain in front of Lori, because she always seemed to be in control and so strong. I didn't want her to think of me as weak.

Her birthday came. February 9th. Also another court date for Janene. Nothing happened that day either. Another waste of the court's time and the tax payers money. I had asked Lori to go to lunch after court. I'd buy her lunch for her 40th birthday. We went to Pizza Hut and had a nice lunch and a nice visit. I didn't speak of my grief, even though it was right there... right at the surface ready to come boiling over. After lunch she brought me home and we came inside. She was sitting on the sofa and I started to go to the dining room and Reggie (our doggie) got under my feet and I lost my balance and fell like a tree in that front room floor. I never could fall gracefully. Lori just started laughing so hard and by then I was pretty sure I hadn't broken anything so I was laughing so hard I couldn't get up. It felt good to laugh and to laugh so spontaneously, but at the same time I felt guilty for laughing when my Troy was lying in his grave.

On Saturday, Bill and Bernie, Lori, Todd and Nicki and I all went to pick out a monument for our Troy. Todd, Nicki and I were riding with Lori and she started telling them about me falling so 'ungracefully' in the front room on Thursday and we were all cracking up. When we pulled in the drive, Lori went to get out of the van and she caught her foot on something and she went out head first, landing on all fours. Oh my God... we just all burst into the loudest laughter. I said, "See what you get for laughing at me? Troy did that to you, ya' know?" I couldn't believe that we were outside the monument place laughing so very hard, but I have to admit that once again it felt good to laugh with my children, if it weren't for the guilt I also felt.

We chose a black stone and wanted a scenery sketched on it with ducks in the foreground on a small pond, a deer by the grove of trees and a Pepsi Truck driving down the road. We had "You touched more lives than you ever knew" inscribed across the bottom and had his picture put at the top with his name and birth date and date of death. On the back it would simply say, Britany and Jessica's dad. It turned out beautiful.

After choosing the monument I went back to Lori's with the kids. We decided to get pizza for supper and Jessica came over too. Larry was working over time. While there that evening we told Lori of the surprise party that didn't happen and I told her about the slideshow I had made. I said, "If you want I will have Todd run me down to get your DVD and we can watch it. When Lori found out that Janene had also spoiled her surprise 40th birthday party, she said, "Just one more reason for me to hate her."

Todd and I went to my house and got the DVD's I had made of Lori's slideshow. We put it in and began to watch it. As soon as the first picture of the 'three' of them came up, Todd broke down and could barely stand to see it. He said he doesn't ever want a picture of just him and Lori in it. Right then, I felt the same way. I had wanted to get a picture of me and my three children taken professionally before it came my time to die, since Todd was back in the area. Janene took that away from me by murdering Troy. I never thought that he would be the one to be taken before me.

Lori said she liked the slideshow. It's so hard for me to

165

watch it with all the pictures of her and her two brothers. Plus, I feel so bad that Troy never got to see it.

For the next couple weeks my emotions were up and down. More down than up. I couldn't get through one hour, never mind one day, without the tears flowing. Lori still didn't want to hear about my grief. I think she thought I would go into such a state of depression that I wouldn't come back from it. By her being so strong and not tolerating my selfish grief, she felt she was not feeding into my despair. Grief is selfish, if you really think about it. Troy is in a place much better than I could ever imagine, but I still grieve because I miss his earthly being. I am grieving for my loss, not his gain.

To me, it appeared she had no grasp of what her dad and I were going through. If you aren't the parent, I guess you can not grasp it. As much as you feel you understand, it simply is not possible to understand the grief of losing a child , never mind losing a child so violently.

To quote from my web site I built in memory of Troy, where I speak of the loss a parent feels...

"We are angry because a very precious human being was ripped from our lives much too soon and much too suddenly and much too tragically. Parents get angry when their child is taken from them. We get angry because that is not the natural order of things. And we are angry even at the person who left us. A grieving parent makes no sense, because they are so mixed up about life that there is no sense to be made from a tragedy such as this.

It's only natural for a grieving parent to think about, cry about, talk about the child that is no longer here. We are so afraid of forgetting what they look like... what they sound like... what they mean in our lives... who they are... and we can not let their memory die with them. We become obsessed with remembering every little detail about them... because it's our way of keeping them alive. We don't want to let go. It's too hard for a parent to think of letting go forever... for an eternity."

Why Lori, a mother couldn't at least in part understand what we were going through, I do not know. But, I can't blame her either, because as much empathy as I had felt in the past for parents who had lost a child, I really had not a clue as to the pain and suffering it caused them. You can't know unless you have walked in their shoes, and I wouldn't wish that on my worst enemy.

March 2nd, Janene was in court again. Once again it was continued. June 27th was the next court pre-trial. It was all so frustrating.

March 6th was fast approaching. My sweet Troy's birthday. I wanted balloons and lots of them to celebrate his life. I found out from Troy's dad that they would be letting go thirty-five balloons on that Sunday, March 5th so that Britany and Jessica could be there. I had typed up little pieces of paper saying, "In Memory Of Troy Patton. Please contact Lola Cross (with my phone and address) if you find this balloon." I never heard back from anyone.

I was beside myself with grief. The fact that Lori didn't seem to even want to try and deal with the overwhelming pain I was in, was only compounding every dark feeling I was having. I had decided I would not go out to the cemetery on that Sunday afternoon. I would wait until Monday, March 6th—Troy's real birthday. I couldn't help but to wonder if it entered Lori's mind what Troy's birthday meant to me. Since she is a mom too, did she know that it took me back to the day he was born and I held him in my arms that first time? Oh God, how I missed my sweet boy. The pain was swallowing up my very being.

Troy's dad called me and told me that he would really like it if I would come out to the cemetery with them for letting the balloons go. I finally told him I would, because I did want to be there for my granddaughters. But, before I could hang up he said, "Now, you know that there's going to be some of Troy's friends out there and we'll be having a beer with Troy for his birthday." I don't know why that effected me so much at that moment. I had thought this was something that was being done for Troy's daughters. How could they feel it was proper to pay tribute to their daddy by standing out there drinking and most likely pouring beer on his grave? To me, that was not for Troy's girls. I didn't want them to think that pouring beer on their daddy's grave was the way to show him respect. Didn't anyone know that where Troy is now, he doesn't want a beer? I got angry. I said, "There you go again. I will not be a part of using beer to pay tribute to my son. I am not going." And I didn't go. I sat here and wept the whole afternoon, because I wanted to be with my granddaughters, but I just couldn't be a part of using beer as a tribute to their daddy. My grief was encompassing my heart and soul and I had no rational thoughts anymore. I only had pain and sorrow.

On March 6th, I had Larry stay home from work, because I honestly didn't trust myself to be alone with my grief. We went and bought some big balloons that said *Happy Birthday* and *I Love You* and we went to the cemetery. As soon as we got past the last row of trees heading out Route 136, we could see Troy's grave and there were so many bright balloons of all colors whipping in the wind. It literally took my breath away and the tears flowed. We went and added our balloons to the rest. All alone. No fanfare. No beer to drink to my son. Just tears and a soft spoken, "Happy Birthday, my sweet Troy. I love you and miss you so much." After a few moments, Larry had to bring me home and I spent the rest of the day crying. It seemed the longer time went, the harder it was getting. I guess because I couldn't pretend anymore that he would be back.

My emotions were still on a roller coaster and what I perceived as Lori not caring about me eating away at my heart. It only pulled me deeper into that black hole I was dwelling in.

About four days before Mother's Day I received an e-mail from her. She wrote that e-mail in response to all the hateful things I said to her, because I simply could not, and still to this day do not remember her hugging me.

She simply told me that she didn't feel I was the mother and grandmother I should be.

Those words cut into the very core of my being.

As you can imagine, I felt the relationship between Lori and I was at rock bottom. And so was I.

It wasn't just her I was lashing out at. I was angry at the whole world and everyone in it. My son had been murdered in an unspeakable way and I couldn't stand it. If Larry would say anything to me, I would often yell at him saying, "You don't know how I feel. He wasn't your flesh and blood. He was MY son!" I really don't know how Larry stuck by me, because I was not me. He often told me with tears rolling down his cheeks that he felt like Janene not only murdered Troy, she had also murdered his wife She had murdered the 'me' I used to be. How very sad that I put Larry through all that. It wasn't his fault and he did love Troy and missed him terribly.

The first Mother's Day without Troy was coming. I literally spent several days crying all day long. I had never felt so all alone. I didn't sleep. I didn't eat. I was at the lowest point in my life and for the first time, even though I had been diagnosed years before with depression, I was seriously contemplating suicide. The pain of Troy being murdered and having to face the fact that I was not the mother or grandmother I should have been was more than I could handle. I was teetering on the edge. Todd would call me and tell me, "Mom, you and Lori are going to destroy this family. You have to talk." He was trying to help I know... but, finally I told him. "Todd, you have to stop trying to be a counselor for Lori and I. If we get counseling we have to get it from someone a little more neutral than you. I feel like if Lori doesn't have her hand on my back pushing me over the edge, then you do."

I told Lori not to get me a Mother's Day present or a card. You can't wish a Happy's Mother's Day to a mom, with her youngest son lying dead in his grave for less than four months.

I stayed in seclusion every day when Larry was working. No lights. No television. No e-mails. I didn't answer my phone. I didn't do anything but cry and try to decide how and where I wanted to do it. I had lost two of my babies, Mother's Day was coming and all I could think of was how badly I wanted to die. Even when Todd came over the day before Mother's Day, I was sitting in the dark sobbing. My heart was broken. I only let him in because he didn't deserve NOT to be let in.

Lori had said in that letter that she thought it was 'high time' she told me the truth. I could only think, "Perfect timing Lori. My son was murdered the day before my birthday and four days before Mother's Day, you decide to tell me that I am not the mom and grandmother you feel I should be." Happy Mother's Day Mom!

She was right. I did love them, but it wasn't enough. I couldn't save Troy and I destroyed my relationship with her without even realizing it.

I don't know how I got through that Mother's Day without going to be with my son. My heart and my mind were consumed with the thought that I wanted to be lying in that grave next to Troy. I felt I couldn't stand one more minute, never mind one more hour of the pain in my heart. I honestly didn't know I could hurt that bad and not die physically from the sheer agony of it. If I went to be with Troy, I wouldn't have to feel the grief and the hurt. I wanted to do it. I wanted to leave this world and leave it on that day. On Mother's Day! I even got in the car with my pills and a soda and started to go to the cemetery, then turned around and came back. I knew if I went out there, the chances would be greater that I would go through with the unthinkable, because each time I see that grave where my son lies, I am overpowered with grief and scream out in pain. It's just too hard to go there and be able to cope with the unimaginable loss of my son.

When I look back on it now, I can only believe that my friends and God saved me. I knew they would all be praying for me fervently on that Mother's Day, because they knew how hard it would be on me. And they didn't even know about Lori and I. They just knew, being mothers themselves, that to lose a child and face that first Mother's Day would be any mom's worst nightmare. So they prayed for me all day long. God heard their prayers and even though nobody else was here to put their arms around me, He was. He had to have held me in His arms to get me through it, because I sure couldn't have done it alone. Thank you friends and thank you God.

I began to realize that if I let this rift between Lori and I continue to grow, then Janene would have won. She would have torn our family apart and I would not give her that satisfaction. Little by little things started getting better and I fought hard to let go of the bad feelings I had. I am still dealing with my grief, and will be for a long time to come. I just can't multiply that pain with the pain of the hurt feelings between Lori and I. Besides, I love my daughter with all my heart too, and if it had been her that had died in some way... then it would have been her that I would be experiencing unspeakable grief over and who knows what would have happened between Troy and I? Or even Todd and I?

I don't know why I do not remember Lori hugging me during that five days. More than once she hugged me. I can not remember it and I sure wish I could. But if she says she did, then I know she did because she would not lie about that. If I could only remember, it would help me so very much.

Bill and I are still the one's suffering the most from our grief. I think that's natural. Troy was our son. The pain of losing a child is beyond description. I remember one time while in Colorado, reading a quote from I think, President Roosevelt where he said, "The beauty of Colorado bankrupts the English language." That's how I feel about the grief of losing a child. That kind of grief also bankrupts the English language.

Right now, we are going into November and we find ourselves in tears more and more as the holidays approach. I don't know how we will get through December and January this first year. But, I have to believe that we will get through it. With the help and love of our remaining children and grandchildren. They are why we have to make it.

Don't ever underestimate the power of grief and anger and what it can do to those left behind. It can either bring you together or tear you apart.

I choose to have what's left of my family, together.

Troy, Mom, Lori and Todd

CHAPTER

12

The Fear — The Signs — The Dreams

You have just read how losing a loved one can take over and almost destroy a family When the death is caused by violence it can cause even more repercussions.

Troy being taken from us by a shotgun blast to the head, was more traumatic than we had yet realized. For all of us. Both the young and the older.

Todd's boy's became afraid to sleep in their own rooms and would come into their mom and dad's room and sleep on the floor with sleeping bags. The oldest was afraid of going past a window at night with the curtains open, because he feared seeing her outside with a gun. Todd had an eerie feeling about coming home from his third shift job and going to sleep, if his wife was gone for the day. It was quite some time before the boys would sleep in their own rooms and understandably so.

Lori, who always gets up about 4:45 a.m. to get both her little ones up, fed, dressed and ready to go to the babysitter's and her go to work, became afraid of going downstairs by herself each morning. She would wake her husband and ask him to go downstairs with her. She got frightened if she was leaving her house alone in the evenings after dark, when she went out to get in the van. Your little brother being murdered is going to affect you in ways you never imagined. Even though we knew she was locked up, there was still that eerie frightening thought of her pulling that trigger.

For quite some time, I would go to sleep with a lamp on in the bedroom. To have someone murdered effects *everyone* that knew that person—family *and* friends. Nobody expects to be going through the murder of someone they know... never mind someone they love with all their hearts.

It was after the inquest that the fear really hit me. I had decided that I needed to see the layout of the house. I hadn't been in that section of the house for more than two years and I felt I needed to see it and get the picture in my mind that the investigator talked about at the inquest. Lori said she thought it was a mistake, but she knew I would argue with her, so Larry and I met her over there and went through the scenario that we had heard. I seemed fine while I was there. Didn't even break down, partly because I didn't want Lori to think bad of me. But at least three times after that day I had nightmares of Janene being in our house with a shotgun and woke Larry up because I was crying out and terrified that she was going to shoot us too.

One evening Lori had her two youngest upstairs getting them ready for bed. Her son hollered for his daddy who was down in the kitchen. His daddy couldn't hear him from there so didn't answer him. Suddenly, Lori's little boy just started screaming and crying and went hysterical because he thought someone had shot his daddy. Troy came running up the stairs the same time Lori got to him and they held him and told him he didn't have to be afraid, because nobody shot his daddy. How very sad that children so young were effected by that evil woman's actions. I know that would have hurt Troy to see that from Heaven.

Speaking of Troy seeing from Heaven. I am convinced that he sees and watches over us all the time. He gives us signs, if only we see them. Maybe I'm just more open to that sort of thing. Actually, I think the signs probably come through God from Troy.

The very first sign was when the lead car in the funeral procession had a dead battery in it. I spoke of that in an earlier chapter. We all felt Troy had a hand in that for sure. It would be just like something he would do. One last prank.

I had little signs around here. For one thing I have some stuffed animals and two angel figurines sitting on the floor in front of our entertainment center. There was one angel in a sitting position with it's legs pulled up, his elbow on his knee and his head resting in his hand. I found that angel twice, turned around sitting backwards facing the wall unit. No way could Reggie, our dog do that. After the second time of finding that angel like that, I took it out to the cemetery and it sits at Troy's grave now.

Then one day, I was talking to a girlfriend on the phone and Reggie was sitting in the dining room staring into the front room and she just kept yapping every few seconds. She never does that, but she just kept acting like she was seeing something. Finally I got up and walked in there to see what she was looking at. I didn't see any activity, but I did find my stuffed gorilla lying in the middle of the front room floor on it's back with it's legs sticking straight up in the air. Guess what it was holding? A small plastic Coca Cola bottle! Troy was a Pepsi Man.

Many times we would go to the cemetery and just as we would pull in, the song 'Believe' by Brooks and Dunn would come on. We had that played at Troy's funeral.

One day I was cleaning through my computer mess here and I came across a brown envelope with nothing written on it. I stuck my hand in it and pulled out the contents. Much to my shock, it was Troy and Janene's wedding pictures. Pictures of their first wedding, at the church. I thought I had gotten rid of all the pictures of her in the house. I was shocked and I was crying to see my boy's face in those photos. I spent a couple hours sitting here looking at them over and over. Not because she was in them, but because they had my son in them. I was noticing the look of love in his eyes for her. But, ultimately I knew I could not keep those photos, even though they had my precious son in them. I asked Larry if he would burn those photos for me. I went out back and sat down in our yard swing and watched as Larry took each photo separately and put them in the small fire he had going. I could see my son's face in those photos from where I was sitting and tears were streaming down my face as they turned to nothing but burned ash. Suddenly, Larry began yelling and yipping and jumping around, "Ouch! That hurts!" He was jumping around in his flip flops like an old hillbilly doing the clog or something, because a hot ash had lit on his big toe and was burning it. I began to laugh so hard at that hilarious sight. I said, "Larry, don't make me laugh so hard when I'm crying... that's mixed emotions!" By then he had come and sat down beside me. I was still laughing when I looked at him and said, "Troy did that to you. He didn't hurt you did he?" I'm convinced that was Troy's way of letting me know it was alright to burn those pictures. It certainly worked. It dried up my tears, except for the ones I was crying from laughing so hard.

April 1st of this year was Jessica's 12th birthday. Troy's baby was going to have her first birthday without her daddy being here. I admit it. I was in tears all day long, just thinking of him not being here for his baby. His ex wife, Jessica's mom said she broke down several times herself. One of my friends said to me that day, "Lola, Troy will let you know somehow that he is there for his daughter's birthday." I thought, "Boy, I certainly hope so. That would be great to get a sign." Her birthday was at the bowling alley and of course the kids all bowled first. Then the candles were lit on her cake and everyone was singing Happy Birthday to Jessica. Suddenly all the lights went out for about five seconds and right back on. I literally let out a gasp, I was so astounded by it. I told Jessica's mom Lisa, "That was Troy. What better time to let her know he is here than while her candles are lit and we are singing to her." Both of us cried we were so moved and touched by it. Larry did go check with the manager just to make sure he hadn't done it, and he had NOT. It was my baby letting his baby know that he was watching over her. He was wishing her a Happy Birthday the only way he could.

One of the most awesome signs I had came to me while I was all alone in the car! For about eight years I had been afraid of driving out on the road. If I had someone with me, I'd drive anywhere, but by myself I just couldn't do it. I had a panic attack one day while driving to a neighboring town, and it scared me so bad that I just wouldn't drive by myself again. Well, Larry and I had gotten new glasses. I had to wait a week and half for mine to come in. It was a Saturday afternoon and Larry was working. I came in from the grocery store and it was around 1 p.m. I had a message on my phone saying that my glasses were in and that they would be closing at 3 p.m. since it was a Saturday. I really did want those glasses and Larry wouldn't even be home until after 4 p.m., and Pekin was forty miles away.

I said to myself, "Lola, you can do this. You can get in that car and drive to Pekin alone to get your glasses. You used to drive there all the time." So, I got the keys and went out and got in the car and took off for Pekin. By the time I got to the edge of town and the viaduct you cross to leave the city limits, I was already stressing out and the panic was building. My chest muscles were tightening and my breathing becoming quick and shallow. As I headed up the incline to cross the viaduct, I said out loud, "Troy baby. Let me know you are with me and I'm not in this all alone, because I don't want to be a wuss about it." I swear with God as my witness, I no sooner spoke those words and the DJ on the radio said, "Soon as we come back, 'One More Day' by Diamond Rio." My mouth must have fell open. We played that song at my baby's funeral. I was astonished by this obvious sign that my son was indeed with me. I listened to the song before I got on my cell phone and tried to call Todd. I couldn't get Todd. I called Lori. I had to tell someone about this biggest and most awesome sign of all that I had received. So, here I was driving down the blacktop, crying with joy, talking on the phone and going around a 45 mph curve at almost 60 mph. I told Lori I had to go before I did wreck the car. Then I said to Troy... out loud again... "Troy, that might have been a bit too big of a sign. I don't think it's good for your mom to be driving down the blacktop crying her heart out." The memory of that will stick with me forever. After that I just sat back and drove all relaxed and literally felt like Troy was sitting right there in the passenger seat with me. I have driven to Pekin on several occasions since. And I don't ask for any signs now, because I already know he is with me.

Three weeks after Troy was murdered, there was a woman from Havana also murdered. Her estranged boyfriend was arrested on three counts of first degree murder, for stabbing her with brut force in the neck, and severing her carotid artery, her larynx and esophagus. The knife nearly went all the way through her neck. His trial started the week of September 18th. I attended that trial every day from the beginning. Starting out, I wanted to see how a murder trial is handled, since some day we would be going through one, too. The first day the jury was picked and one witness testified. The next morning when I entered the court room, I sat in the same area I had the day before. Then I realized that Stephanie's family and friends were all sitting on the other side of the room and I didn't want them to think I was there in support of her alleged killer, so I got up and moved to the other side of the court room and sat with them. From that moment on, I was there in support of Steph's family. By noon on Friday, September 22nd the jury went into deliberation. I left that court house totally convinced in my mind and heart that yes, he was guilty. I headed straight to the cemetery and I stood at my son's grave and cried, partly because I had been so stressed during the whole trial, because I knew how hard it had to be on her family. I said to my boy, "Troy, Steph's family is about to get justice for her, and we will get justice for you too. I promise you that."

After a little more than five hours of deliberating, the jury came back with a 'guilty' verdict! Even though

I missed the actual verdict being read, I was there in the parking lot to hug Steph's family and let them know I cared and was happy that they got their justice. As Larry and I were leaving the parking lot to go home, I looked up in the sky and I said, "Larry, look at that. A double rainbow. One for Steph and one for Troy." I believe those were a sign from my son to let me know that he and God were watching, and we'd get justice too. I had goose bumps and was moved to tears. And on November 2nd, 2006, Trent Elliot was sentenced to forty-two years in prison, of which he will have to spend one hundred percent of that time. He'll be seventy-eight years old, before he gets out. Thank You God!

I have always believed that if you dream of someone who has passed on, it is God's way of letting you visit that person for a little while. I feel no differently about that now that I have lost my son.

On October 28th, I had what was and will probably remain one of the most vivid dreams I've had since Troy's death.

I didn't go to bed until 4 a.m. because I was working on a web page for the web site I have built in memory of my son. While sleeping I dreamed of my Troy. It was the most vivid dream I have had. In my dream it was Troy's birthday and God had decided that there had been a mix up and he was gonna let our Troy come back to us for one more day. We were having a birthday party for him and were all gathered here at our house, which really wasn't our house at all. It was more like a school cafeteria or something. Bill and I had both bought gifts for Troy and I had written a couple short poems and attached to the birthday bag, to make it a bit more special. Larry was in another room and was the first to see Troy. Troy, in his usual character put his finger to his mouth, signaling to Larry that he was going to surprise his dad and I. Next thing we knew there was our Troy. Bill was closest and grabbed him first to hug him. Oh dear God, he looked so good. He was so happy and had his camouflage cap on like in the picture I love of him where he's smiling so big. When Bill took his arms away, I was waiting right there to grab my sweet Troy and hug him like there was no tomorrow. Because in fact, there wasn't going to be a tomorrow and we knew that. As I was hugged my Troy, he gave me a big ol' bear hug back—so I think Heaven took away his reluctance to give big ol' hugs in public. Suddenly I woke and there I was in my own bed and Troy wasn't there at all. I cried out in the most agony, "No, no, no... Troy come back. Please Troy. Don't leave us now!" I was crying so hard I couldn't stop for the longest time. I thought to myself, what a cruel dream to have. It all seemed so real only to wake and realize that he is still gone. When I calmed down, I told Larry that maybe 'One More Day' as the song says, would not be a good idea, because it hurts too bad to let them go again. I love you my sweet Troy and now that I am calmed down I am thanking God for giving me that chance to hug you one more time, if only in a dream.

On my birthday of this year, January 29th, I cried myself to sleep. I did fairly well the 28th and even on my birthday until I went to bed that night. As soon as my head hit that pillow the tears began to fall. All I could think about was Troy and how we hadn't seen him for a year and how I wished I could see him.

When I finally fell asleep, my pillow wet with tears I dreamed of my Troy. I dreamed I was lying on the couch crying so hard and my friend Dee was here trying to console me. Suddenly there was Troy standing beside me. He was five years old and he looked at me with those big, beautiful blue eyes and he asked, "What's the matter Mom?" I looked at him and I answered, "Oh Troy. I just miss you so much I can't stand it most days." He crawled up on the sofa and wrapped his little arms around my neck and while hugging me said, "Don't worry Mom. I won't ever leave you. I promise."

What a wonderful gift God had given me for my birthday. A visit from my sweet boy. I told Lori and Todd the next day... I think God chose to send Troy to me at five years old because he was so cuddly with me at that age. I also believe the message in what he said to me was that he never will truly leave me, because he lives on in my heart and my memories.

Thank you God for letting me visit my son for my birthday.

I know that as time passes God will send Troy to me in other dreams. He will wait until he knows I need to see Troy the most and there my boy will be. Talking to me and hugging me... if only in my dreams.

Troy 1976

CHAPTER

13

The Trial That Didn't Happen

We had been in court so many times over the almost twelve months since Troy had been brutally murdered. Each time she was in court—WE were in court. We wanted her to have to look at us when she came into that room and not be able to forget for one second what she had done to all of us. Of course, the wheels of the justice system turn very slowly sometimes. Every time we went to court it would only be continued, which meant another three months of waiting, wondering and wanting justice for our Troy.

It seemed that her demeanor changed on different occasions when we would see her in the court room. In the beginning she would be whimpering, avoiding making eye contact with us as much as possible. We always sat straight across from her so that if she looked straight ahead, all of Troy's family and friends were right there facing her. She would fidget in her seat and try to turn her head to look out the window. Partly because she was trying not to look at us... partly because she couldn't see the outside from her cell in the Mason County Jail, so it had to seem somewhat a treat for her to be able to be out of that cell even if it was for a five minute court appearance that inevitably ended in another postponement.

Each time she was brought into court she was wearing her black and white striped uniform and a bullet proof vest. None of the other inmates wore a bullet proof vest. Just her. None of Troy's family would have ever done anything to her, because we are made of different stuff than she is... but, passions ran deep in this town when someone that was so loved was taken out in such a way. People didn't like her before this... they certainly hated her after she murdered Troy. The authorities must have felt the threat level was high because the Sheriff's Department made sure she stayed safe. If only someone could have kept Troy safe. There were two times that I can think of, that they drove her from the Mason County Jail across the street right up to the entrance of the court house. Most of the time they walked her over.

In June when we were in court she had a totally different attitude. We still don't understand why, but that day she just seemed to be all laid back and arrogantly looking us right in the eye after having spent the last five months avoiding our glares. She was sitting back in her chair, leaning to the side actually touching arms with the male inmate sitting next to her. We always wondered if she was sedated on that day, or was it the previous court appearances that she had been sedated? We'll never know why her attitude was different on that day, and I guess it doesn't even matter but it's something I will always wonder about, and I'll never get that look on her face out of my mind.

The State's Attorney had offered Janene a plea agreement of thirty -four years if she'd plead guilty. She was facing life in prison if she went to trial and was found guilty on even one of the three first degree murder charges against her. Her lawyer didn't let her accept that agreement. He probably had to wonder if he'd made the right decision when the other person on trial for murder, Mr. Elliot was found guilty and sentenced to forty-two years in prison for the murder of Stephanie Nicholas. The public defender at one time made a counter offer. He wanted Janene to only spend twenty years in prison in exchange for a guilty plea. Of course, that was not an option we would even entertain and thankfully neither did the State's Attorney. The wheels of justice seemed to almost be coming to a standstill for us. Each time we went to court her lawyer would ask for another continuance.

On December 20th, 2006, just five days before Christmas there had been a pretrial hearing scheduled and the trial was to begin January 8th. We actually hated knowing we would have that hanging over our heads during the holidays. We needn't have worried since on December 20th, her lawyer once again asked for another continuance, only this time he asked that a special jury be convened for a March 19th, 2007 trial date. Normally, a jury is only convened every three months, so since the January 8th trial wasn't to be, that would have put us to April. He also asked that an appearance be set up for January 4th in which he wanted to argue some motions that he would be filing by Friday, December 22nd. Each day I checked with the court house and no motions had been filed. The court house was closed on December 25th, 26th and 27th due to the Christmas Holiday break. I checked late in the afternoon both on December 28th and December 29th and still he had filed no motions. The next week the court house was closed on January 1st and 2nd for the New Year's. We had no idea what to think as to why he hadn't filed the motions that were to be argued on January 4th. Then on the evening of January 3rd my daughter got a surprising phone call from Kristen Miller, the State's Attorney. Roger Thomson, the public defender, had notified her that Janene would be accepting the latest plea agreement. She would plead guilty to the second count of first degree murder and agree to spend thirty years in prison, and be given credit for the almost a year she had already spent incarcerated in the Mason County Jail.

When Troy's family and friends showed up in court on Thursday, January 4th, 2007 her lawyer seemed perturbed that we were there. He said to us that there was not going to be an appearance by Mrs. Patton that morning. (Always made me want to throw up when she was called 'Mrs. Patton'. She doesn't deserve to bear that name.) We assured him that we knew that, but we wanted to be there anyway. He asked if we had talked to Kristen Miller and we said, "yes." He asked when we had last talked to her and my daughter informed him that she had received a call the evening prior. He then went over and said something to the officer in the court room and the court officer said we'd wait until the State's Attorney arrived and see what happened. We had every right to be in that court room that morning. We think that her attorney hated the thought of having to tell the judge that his client was going to plead guilty and take the plea agreement, with us sitting there. He asked that a court date be set up for the last of January or the first part of February. I can't really remember that now. Whatever the date was, the judge said he would not be available on that day so it would be set for January 8th, 2007. We couldn't believe it! In four days it would all be over.

Monday, January 8th by 8:00 a.m., her family and Troy's family and friends were already filling the small court room. At 9 a.m. she was brought in. Shackled, black and white stripes and her bullet proof vest. They had driven her to the door that morning I would find out later. The judge asked her a few questions to make sure she knew and understood what she was about to do and the consequences of pleading guilty. She did understand

and was not on any medication that would hamper her thought process, so her guilty plea was entered. After doing so, she read from a written statement she had prepared. It went as follows.

"Your honor, I've asked myself a million times what to say and I've prayed for God's guidance.

I'm sorry. Those words seem so little to say. I am sorry and wish I could turn back the hands of time, but I can't. I will say I loved my husband dearly and always will. It tears at my heart every minute to know the pain and hurt I've caused to his family, children, friends and all involved.

I have prayed and will carry those prayers with me for God to be there and help to heal all our hurt. I know not one person in this courtroom or those lives Troy touched will ever be the same. If I could bring him back I would. I know doing time is hard, but the hardest thing is knowing the pain I've caused. 'I'm sorry' is all I can say, and I pray that God will carry us all through this."

As you see, we could have written that statement for her, because we knew exactly what she would say. And you notice that she didn't tell us why she murdered my son.

She was then sentenced to the thirty years, with time served being accredited to her and was told she would spend one hundred percent of that time behind bars. She will be locked up in prison until January 28th, 2036. However, she did still have thirty days to change her mind on her guilty plea. She couldn't just change her mind on a whim. She would have had to show 'just cause' for a change of heart in the matter. She didn't use that option. Thank God.

After she was removed from the court house and returned to jail we talked with reporters briefly, and then we told them that we were going to the cemetery. We explained that early on we had promised Jessica, Troy's youngest daughter that when we knew Janene was going to prison, we'd take balloons to her daddy's grave to commemorate that day. We had already ordered thirty red, white and blue balloons to be picked up on the way to my son's grave. Each member of Troy's family and each of his friends that were there, tied a balloon to the Shepard's Hooks that were already there to let the world know that justice had been served for Troy. It was a pretty amazing sight to see those thirty balloons flying in the wind that morning. We cried, we prayed, and we thanked God for keeping us as strong as we could be during such an ordeal. But her guilty plea didn't bring us any kind of joy really. It didn't bring Troy back. That is what I tried to prepare myself for mentally... no matter if she pleaded guilty or was found guilty by a jury... it would not give us our Troy back.

No trial meant no answers to all our questions. That left us with only what we knew from seeing things with our own eyes, and what we were able to learn during the last several months from people that knew both Troy and Janene, newspaper accounts of interviews, the people that witnessed what went on that night and what the doctor had told us that cold January morning before dawn. We pieced it all together although maybe not perfectly, we were very close to the truth of what happened during their marriage and subsequent tragedy.

We had a person tell us that Janene might have been tiny, but she was a 'HELL CAT!' That pretty much summed her up. She was only five foot two inches tall and weighed about one hundred and thirty pounds, although her weight fluctuated a lot... for good reason. Her being only five foot two was probably one thing that attracted Troy to her, because he was of small stature.

She had been in the National Guard and was quite capable of loading a shotgun and was not a weak, timid female by any means. She actually was trained as a medic in the Guard. Somehow I had not ever realized that she had been in the National Guard, so that's why Troy's guns didn't concern me that much, because I didn't think she would know how to load a shotgun.

Her demeanor changed so rapidly at times, because she was heavily into methamphetamine, cocaine, marijuana and of course, she drank alcohol. All of the above showed up in her blood the morning of Troy's murder. We have learned that she did drugs with people that we never would have believed would be partying with her. Some people came right up to my daughter and said, "I have done drugs with Janene." My son had used drugs too, but according to what we have learned, he was more of a recreational user, whereas Janene was an addict.

It hurts a mom to know that her son was using illegal drugs, even on a recreational basis. I would never have thought Troy would do that... but, there's no denying it now. They had found traces of cocaine metabolites in his toxicology tests. He had not used drugs on that night, but he had used them. But alcohol was and always had been his drug of choice. He was NOT addicted to methamphetamine or cocaine! We were assured of that!

We found out when my daughter and son took over

Troy's financial affairs after his death, that she had him in financial ruin. We know he knew some of it, because they had filed bankruptcy on their credit cards at one time. But he had no idea that he was about to lose both houses and both vehicles. As I mentioned in an earlier chapter, Janene had asked a postal employee to hide their mail in the garage so Troy wouldn't see the late payment notices when they came in. I've heard that the mail was hidden from him, and I've heard that it wasn't. I don't know which story is true, but I tend to think it was hidden from him. If he had lived even a couple more weeks or a month at the most, he would have found out that he was about to lose everything.   There had been $22,000 taken out of my son's 401k plan just in the year of 2005. Each slip was signed with Troy's name, but many of them were in Janene's hand writing. We'll never know if Troy knew about the ones she signed his name to. The first week alone after Troy was murdered, Lori received thirteen over draft statements from the bank. Janene had written every one of those checks. Who knows how many others there had been before that. One woman said that the day before Troy was killed he had called their store and told her that he had just found out that they had some checks that came back to the store and he was sorry and he would be in on Saturday to take care of them. He never got that chance.

She was snorting his check, her check, his retirement 401k, and any other money that came into the house right up her nose. That's the only explanation there could be for the shape she had their finances in. Troy trusted her to send the payments off, and she had him believing that she was, when in fact they either weren't getting paid at all or the checks were bouncing like rubber balls right back to the bank.

As I mentioned earlier in Chapter 9, rumors were circulating before she murdered Troy, that she was having an affair with a psych patient in the nursing home where she was employed and that some legal issues were coming up pertaining to her job, the week of January 30th, 2006. We didn't know if those rumors were true, but we didn't doubt for one second that she was capable of carrying on an affair with another man. After Troy was murdered, everything changed so drastically. We were all trying so hard to deal with the shock and grief of it all, that we eventually forgot about those rumors because nothing was ever mentioned about it again.

One day I got an e-mail from a very dear friend. She asked if I had seen the Peoria Journal Star that day. I hadn't, but started thumbing through it immediately. There it was in the August 16th, 2006 issue of the paper.

NURSING HOME FINED OVER SEX RELATIONSHIP

Public Health says Prairie View failed to stop resident, staffer affair

What a slap in the face that was. Almost seven months after she had murdered Troy it was finally made public knowledge that she was having an affair. Of course, the nursing home is appealing that ruling, as it was a $10,000 fine they were hit with. I went online and read the official report of the investigation done by the Illinois Department of Public Health. She had been reported on numerous occasions by other employees, but for whatever reasons, her boss chose to ignore the reports of a sexual relationship going on between Janene and a young resident of the facility. In reading that report I learned that on January 25th, her superiors finally talked with her about this man and their relationship. They talked with her again on Friday, January 27th about it, telling her it had to stop.

Did Troy know about the affair? Guess we will never know now, but we think she had to tell him something. Since she was a habitual liar and would never outright admit to Troy that she was having an affair, she probably told him that something happened, but it was against her will or that other workers were spreading lies about her. She may have told him that the guy sexually attacked her. She might have even told him that she was going to lose her job because of it. We think that may be what had Troy so worried the day his dad saw him in the grocery store not long before his death. There is no way of knowing for sure.

On April 3rd, 2007 pursuant to the Freedom Of Information Act, we were allowed to view the interrogation they did with Janene after she had murdered our Troy. It was done in two segments. The first beginning on the morning of January 28th, 2006 the day she tore our hearts out. The second being on January 29th, my birthday—the day we spent making arrangements to bury our precious Troy. We were to find out during that interrogation that we were right on target with the statements I made in the previous paragraph. No more speculating and trying to piece that part together.

In the beginning of the tape, she had just been told that Troy had died. She was in the corner of the room, screaming and crying and being quite the 'Drama Queen', "Nooooo, he can't be gone. He can't be gone. Nooo, he just can't be gone!"—all the while rocking back and forth in a sitting position on the floor. I really don't doubt that it did upset her terribly that Troy was gone, because that meant she was looking at murder charges. I also feel that even though someone kills another intentionally, it still has to be a very traumatic thing for that person to know that they intentionally caused someone's death—in this case, her own husband's. One of her fears was how her family would feel about her upon hearing she had killed Troy. She seemed to be more worried what they would think, than what we would think. She did however, mention her own children and Troy's girls, even though her thoughts were erratic and nothing too comprehensible was coming out of her mouth at that point. She did say that Troy was her life. She said he loved her kids and they loved him. She just didn't know how her son would handle losing Troy.

You have to understand, at the beginning of the tape, that she had been partying the night before, using drugs and alcohol. She had been up since early the morning prior, with no sleep in over twenty-four hours. She had shot and killed her husband and was coming down from whatever 'high' she had been on. She was not in very good shape. She mentioned more than once that she was going to be sick or that she was dizzy or that she was cold. Each time she would say something like that she was asked if she wanted to stop talking until later. She would agree to go on with the interrogation. She was brought a blanket to wrap herself in to get warm. They got her a roll of paper towels, because they didn't have any tissues. And they brought her water to drink, because her mouth looked dry. She was asked at several different times if she wanted something to eat. She declined any food. They gave her a piece of gum, which later she did chew for a while. She had also been told that she was being taped, both audio and video. But in spite of everything, she just kept talking and talking... almost nonstop. I feel that it was all a part of her need to be the center of attention and Lord knows she had achieved that with the investigators.

Questions of drug use came up, of course. She stated that she never used drugs except with Troy. Not true! But, it was her story, so as the song says, "That's my story and I'm stickin' to it". She said they used cocaine, cannabis and had both tried methamphetamine and liked it too much, so they were in the process of quitting methamphetamine. She claimed that they would buy a half gram of drugs for about $50 and it would last them for a few days. The investigator told her that they knew she did use drugs without Troy, and asked if she'd tell them who she used drugs with. She would rather not say was her answer. She stated that they only used methamphetamine about once a month, since they were both trying to get away from using it. Actually, she said the first time they used it, they didn't even know it was methamphetamine. They thought it was cocaine. Who knows if that was true? I sure don't.

When they got around to her and the resident at her place of employment she was saying that nothing was going on between them. As the investigator pressed on... and it is literally done second by second and he was very skillful at getting to the truth. It's a very long drawn out process and things were went over again and again and again. Eventually, she told them that this man had become fixated with her and she did not realize it. She said she had paid for him some contact lenses at one time and then his dad sent her $250 and she put that in her checking account, so she could just give it to the resident, as he needed it. But when he asked for money for alcohol, she wouldn't give it to him to buy alcohol or drugs because of the medications he was on. Of course, knowing her the way we did, we are certain that once that $250 went into her checking account, it was gone.

She also admitted that she had given this man both her home phone number and cell phone number and he called her at home quite often. And she also called him from home. When asked if she gave all her residents her phone number, she snapped back at him, "No, I didn't. But I cared about this man and worried about him. That's just the way I am, all right? I care about people."

Finally, taking little baby steps with her, the investigator got her to tell more and more. It's pretty amazing to watch how they are trained to make her feel like they understand totally what she was doing and do not blame her or judge her in any way. They built a rapport with Janene, which put her at ease and made it easier for her to talk with them and answer questions.

She slowly started telling how her co-workers were telling her that this man was too attached to her. Eventually, she said that she brought this man into her office and told him that their relationship was strictly professional and that is the way it had to remain.

According to her, he did not take that too well and he wound up raping her right there in her office. She first said he held one hand over her mouth as he pulled his and her pants down. Then she said that he pinned her hands down. First she said that she was facing him when this happened, then she said later that he had turned her around and raped her from behind. Hard to keep a story straight when you're lying. I'm not a rocket scientist, but I would have thought that once he obviously had to remove his hand from her mouth to pin her arms down, that would have been the perfect opportunity to start screaming for help. Wouldn't it? Once this rape had occurred and he left her office, she did nothing. She did not report it to anyone. Except my son. She told him that this man raped her and of course he was devastated by it. His wife had been raped and he was not there to protect her. She admitted that the night they argued before she murdered him that she asked him where the hell he was when she got raped. Well, Troy was at work, just where he was suppose to be. Troy wanted her to report the patient to the authorities and she refused, saying she didn't want the humiliation. Troy was having a hard time dealing with the fact that not only had another man violated his wife, but she would not report this 'supposed' rapist. She had also told Troy that she would probably be losing her job. And that is what was lying so heavily on our son's mind the day his dad saw him in the store. How very sad it makes us to know how burdened his heart was the last few days of his life. I think back to January 26th, when Larry and I last saw him alive. Oh my God, that boy was so good at hiding his feelings. He seemed like the same, happy go lucky, worry free man he always seemed to be. I just break into sobs thinking what all he had on his mind. He deserved so much better.

As the interrogation continued, the investigator asked Janene what she would say if he told her that they found that man's pubic hair in the front seat of her personal van and in the back of the van? She of course was stunned and didn't know what to say when first told of this. But, just as before... second by second... bit by bit the story came out. She told how she had taken this man with her one day on an errand and they had pulled into a tractor trail in a corn field and began to make out. Kissing and hugging. Actually it came out that they had been doing a lot of that, including in her office at work. Anyway, she thought the back of the van would be more comfortable for them, so she had gotten out and folded down the seats and made room for him and her to do their love making in the back of the van. According to her, the guy was unable to perform that day, so they ended up going back to the home without having accomplished any actual intercourse. She claimed that after that incident, she decided that it was wrong. She loved her husband and she had to stop acting like this with the young man. Of course, that part was a lie, as was proved during the investigation. She had promised this man that she would leave her husband and children, and they would be together.

We learned that on January 27th, Troy had met her at her job in Lewistown. They had went to a loan company in Canton and renewed a loan in Troy's name for $700. (Maybe that was money to take care of those bad checks he had promised to take care of on Saturday. The check was still un-cashed and in his wallet when he was murdered the next morning). They then went together to Kewanee to pick up a resident of the nursing home and bring them back to Lewistown. The investigator asked Janene if Troy might have wanted to see this man that had 'raped' her and that's why he went to the nursing home with her? She said Troy already knew the guy because Troy came by her place of employment every day and had lunch with her, since he always came to Lewistown last on his Pepsi job.

Later in the evening, around 8:45 p.m., after they returned with the patient, Troy left the van in the parking lot of the nursing home and they went in the Grand Am to a Lewistown Bar and were having a few drinks with friends. According to the bartender's account of that night, Janene suddenly and without any provocation, became irritated and irrational, yelling at Troy and arguing.

Janene confirmed this account during the interrogation. She said she got angry when she walked by a guy in the bar, whom she didn't like and he obviously didn't like her either because he said to her, "Quit shadowing me, bitch!" She walked away from that man and chose to take it out on Troy.

Troy kept telling her to calm down and just try to enjoy the evening. At one point they went to the end of the bar or outside the bar to the Beer Garden, she couldn't remember that part too well, but Janene threw a beer bottle at my son, breaking it. Eventually, right before closing time, Janene left the bar. Troy was going to walk from the bar to the nursing home to get the van. Janene drove around the block and came back and picked him up and took him to get the van. They both drove home, the ten miles or so from there, both too intoxicated to be driving. They didn't take the same route home according to Janene, because she didn't see Troy's lights behind her as she drove. When she got almost to the Havana Bridge she pulled down into a dirt road that goes down into the river bottoms. She said she did this to just sit there and think and also because she wanted to make sure Troy was okay. He did come down the highway and saw her pulled off the road and pulled in behind her and asked her what the hell she was doing there. She had gotten out of her vehicle and in her anger threw her car keys and cell phone at Troy. He, probably because he was intoxicated, drove away and went on home. She claimed she then realized that she didn't have any keys because she had thrown them inside the van. She got on Troy's phone he used for his Pepsi sales job and called the house phone. Troy answered and she told him he had to bring her keys to her, so she could get home. He told her he didn't have them, and she told him, that they were in the van. He drove back to where she was, and she found the keys between the door and the front drivers seat. Both drove back to town, with Troy arriving first. Janene pulled in the drive at an excessive speed (according to witnesses next door), and acted as though she was going to hit Troy with the car. She got out and the arguing continued in the driveway of their home. Neither of them were aware that three people next door were watching the whole scene play out. Janene was hitting Troy and cursing loudly at him. He backed away from her and kept asking her to calm down.

Those three witnesses said, as did the bartender in

Lewistown that Troy did not ever raise a hand to her during all the arguing and her hitting on him. And when the investigator asked Janene over and over at different times during the interrogation, "Did Troy hit you? Did Troy slap you?" her answer was always the same. Troy had never hit her. Not that night and not on any other occasion that she had physically abused him. She even repeated several times that Troy was a good man. He wouldn't hurt anyone or hit her.

I felt both proud and sad at the same time when I heard that.

She went on to say that, at one point she got in the car and left the premises. She drove down to the river and sat for a few seconds and returned. Before going into the house, she stopped to continue the arguing briefly, which was all about the man that raped her and her not reporting him to authorities. "I couldn't take the way Troy looked at me—like I was a disgrace." she put it. She also said Troy called her the 'C' word and that really angered her and that he knew it would, when he said it. At that time she went into the house with the intentions of ending it all.

It was at this time that she was asked if that's the first time she ever threatened suicide. She said she had threatened that while married to her second husband. The investigator pointed out that a woman who commits suicide, doesn't usually use a gun and especially not a shotgun. They lean more towards an overdose of pills or car accident or something like that. He asked what she was going to use when she threatened suicide with her second husband. She said it was a pistol but she didn't think it was even loaded.

Noting that they had gotten off the track a little bit, he asked her to continue with her story. She continued, saying she went to the gun cabinet, which she first said was unlocked. Later she changed that part of her story and admitted that it was locked and she had to climb up and get the key out of a stein on the top. She kept talking, "I tried to load one shotgun. For some reason, I couldn't get the shell in it. I threw it down and took the second gun out and loaded it." According to her, she was going to end her life because she just couldn't handle it... "That look in his eyes. Just the way he looked at me." she repeated more than once.

After loading the shotgun, she went to the sliding doors that lead onto the small deck. She opened the door and stepped outside, pointing the gun at Troy. Witnesses told that part. She said she just opened the door, and because the gun was so long, they probably saw the barrel of it sticking out the door and that she did not point it at Troy.

The three people watching said when Troy saw the gun pointed at him, he put his hands in the air as one would do when a gun is pointed at you. She told him she was going to end her life. She said his response was, "You might as well end mine, too." She went into the house to the bathroom, locking the sliding doors behind her. Sometime during all this she had taken her blouse and bra off. She didn't remember when or why she did that. She said she must have been going to put her pajamas on.

"You wanted to be in your pajamas when you killed yourself?"

"I don't know what I thought," she answered.

207

She sat down on the toilet to pee.

Again the investigator questioned her, "Were you going to shoot your self while sitting on the toilet?" She actually kind of chuckled at that, and said, "That's when I realized that it was kind of crazy for me to think I could shoot myself in the head with a shotgun, because it's so big and I'm so short. I changed my mind about committing suicide and decided to put the gun back in the cabinet."

During all of that scenario, which was a pretty short time span, Troy was on the outside of the house trying to break the door in to get to that woman and save her life... just like she knew he'd do. According to the witnesses who were at least forty feet away in an enclosed glassed in porch, it took Troy three or four tries to kick that door in and the noise was almost as loud as the gunshot they would hear in a matter of a couple minutes at the very most.

In the meantime, according to Janene, she exited the bathroom still holding the gun with both hands. As she walked into the dark hallway, she caught a glimpse of a shadowy figure moving in their darkened bedroom doorway. It startled her and she jumped and having her finger on the trigger, the gun just went off. She couldn't believe that she pulled the trigger. And she still didn't know it was Troy. She went to the bedroom where this strange intruder lay in his own blood and reached in and turned on the light. That's when she saw it was Troy and started screaming for help.

Little by little, just as before, the truth started coming out. The investigator asked her, "Janene, how could you not hear Troy breaking in the door? You were only, at the most, twenty feet from that door. It was loud!" His voice bellowed as he banged his fist three times on the table saying, "Boom! Boom! Boom!" Visibly shaken and even angry, she retorted, "The dog was barking. That's why I didn't hear Troy breaking in the door! I did NOT know my husband was in the house!" The investigator asked, "How can a dog that tiny possibly bark so loud, that you wouldn't hear someone kicking three or four times to break down a door not twenty feet away?" "Oh, that dog can bark, let me tell you." was her reply. The interrogation continued and the story started changing again.

He then brought up her going to the bedroom to turn on the light, when she didn't know if this strange intruder was dead, alive, or had a gun? "How did you know that he wouldn't grab you when you went to that bedroom door?" He asked, " When you shot this stranger in your dark bedroom, why wouldn't you have been so scared that you would have went running outside to your husband, who according to you was still outside?"

She then began to slowly change her story, again when he asked, "Isn't it true that your husband had turned the light in the bedroom on, Janene?" She said, "Well, as soon as I shot him, HE turned on the bedroom light and I saw that it was my husband." The investigator questioned, "Janene, you were a medic in the Army National Guard. You know that when you shot Troy, you shot him in the right side of his head and the bullet exited the back of his skull taking part of the brain stem with it. You know that once that shot hit, Troy would not have been able to turn the light on or do anything else. He would have instantly lost all ability to do anything."

Her story changed even more. " I think he had already turned the light on, but he turned it on the same time I shot and it was too late. I saw it was Troy, but I had already pulled the trigger. I still can't believe I pulled the trigger. I can't believe I pulled the trigger."

The truth had finally been reached.

Troy had broken down the door to get in to save her from suicide. He went through the kitchen and TV room area, more than likely calling out her name as he did so. He got to the bedroom door and reached in behind the dresser with his left hand to turn the light switch on. As the light came on and he turned towards the hallway, she was standing in wait, just a few feet from him, with a shotgun aimed at his head.

She pulled the trigger!

It lifted so much anguish from my heart for me to hear that the instant he was shot, Troy knew nothing, felt nothing, said nothing... all he could do was fall down.

She blew him straight to Heaven.

Final resting place for Troy Patton. Laurel Hill Cemetery, Havana, IL..

Murderer!!!

God didn't pull that trigger
It wasn't in his plan
For you to load a shotgun
And kill that gentle man

He was a trusting husband
As he took you for his wife
Never did he dream
You would take his life

You lied, used drugs and cheated
Satan lives within your heart
Together with the Devil
You tore my world apart

Your wicked ways were lethal
You had nowhere to run
So for just a little money
You blew away my son

He was a Dad to Brit and Jess
Todd and Lori's little brother
A special son to four of us
And loved by many others

The pain is so unbearable
We miss him more each day
All because you took a gun
And blew my son away

Lola Cross
4/12/06

R80805 - PATTON, JANENE L.

CONCLUSION

Trying to Understand

Britany, Troy and Jessica in 2004

My heart is so broken that I have no idea how I can go on breathing. I can only believe that God wants me to remain here for a reason. I go to the cemetery and my world shatters again, because I can't put my arms around a grave. I feel I can not stand one more second of knowing that he is gone! Then the next thing I know another day has passed by without him. I don't understand in my heart why the world keeps on turning when someone so special has been taken out of it in such an unspeakable, evil way.

And then on top of the unbearable pain... there is the over powering anger! What she has done to this family was the unthinkable before that day.

We all get up each day. We put one foot in front of the other and go through the motions, all the while with Troy in our hearts and minds. Still unable to believe that she ripped him from our lives. It's the most horrific pain that anyone can imagine. Only through the help of each other and the grace of God are we even slightly able to live life this day or any day since January 28th, 2006. And so I write. I write about my Troy and I write about my pain. It helps me to talk about him. It helps me to look at his pictures. I want to remember each and every little thing about him. A very big part of me and all of us, died that day with my son.

God chose to take him from us quickly. I try to tell myself that God knew what He was doing, and I honestly do believe He did. Troy would not have wanted to be different than he ever was. If he couldn't be him... he would choose not to 'be'. And Troy, as much as it breaks my heart... I'm trying to understand.

217

Mom and Troy

I'M LEFT HERE MISSING YOU

I know you must be watching
As I struggle here below
You see my heart was shattered
When I had to let you go

If you could only speak
And tell me why it had to be
Why HE called you home
Instead of taking me

If your work on earth is done
Then what's left for me to do
There has to be a reason
I'm left here missing you

Was I left behind for now
So I can share your story, Troy
Or is it something else
Please tell me, my sweet boy

I want the world to know
That within the little man
There lived a gentle giant
Always there to lend a hand

I'm telling your life's story
A little at a time
I want everyone to know
I love you... son of mine

Love,
Mom
November 10, 2006

219

About the Author

Lola Cross was born in 1947 to Samuel and Lola Taylor. She grew up in the small central Illinois town of Delavan and graduated high school there in 1965. She has a total of seven siblings—two sisters and one brother who grew up in the same home with her. One sister and one brother grew up in her maternal grandparents home. She also had two half sisters, born to her dad and his second wife that she reconnected with a few years ago.

Her biggest desire in childhood was to grow up, get married and have children. She knew at a very young age that she wanted a daughter and that she would name her Lori. Lola married right out of high school and had three children.

Most people would agree that she was not known for anything special. She felt she was known as something very special... Lori, Todd and Troy's mom. That was the most important thing she could be known as, and still is.

From the time Lola was a young teenager she would express her feelings in her writing—sometimes in the form of poems. Any time something would affect her in a really emotional way, she would go to her room, turn on her 45 rpm record player and write until she had gotten it all out of her system and could cry no more.

It is from that form of handling stress and sadness that this book was born.

GET HELP
GET INFORMED
GET INVOLVED

STOPFAMILYVIOLENCE.ORG

Every year millions of people are abused in this country. Stop Family Violence is a leading national organization working to bring survivor voices - and the voices of their allies - to bear on the social and political agendas affecting their lives.

Mission: *Stop Family Violence's mission is to organize and amplify our nation's collective voice against family violence. We are a catalyst for social change - empowering people to take action at the local, state and national level to ensure safety, justice, accountability and healing for people whose lives are affected by violent relationships. Our goal is family peace.*

Published by stopfamilyviolence.org May 1st 2007

Printed in the United States
85326LV00001BA/4-18/A

9 780979 527616